Contents

Part I: Identifying Your Institution's Image

Part II: Creating an Image Program

Part III: Marketing and Institutional Image

Part IV: Appendix

Institutional Image: How to Define, Improve, Market It

Robert S. Topor

Council for Advancement and Support of Education

ISBN 0-89964-242-X

Printed in the United States of America.

The Council for Advancement and Support of Education (CASE) provides books, art packages, microfiche, and focus issues of the monthly magazine, CURRENTS, for professionals in institutional advancement. The books cover topics in alumni administration, creative communications, fund raising, government relations, institutional relations, management, publications, and student recruitment. For a copy of the catalog RESOURCES, write to the CASE Publication Order Department, 80 South Early Street, Alexandria, VA 22304.

Book design by Richard Rabil
Cover illustration by Michael David Brown

Council for Advancement and Support of Education
Suite 400, 11 Dupont Circle, Washington, DC 20036

"There is danger
in reckless change; but greater danger
in blind conservatism."
—*Henry George*

Acknowledgements

A warm handshake and special note of thanks to the people at the Council for the Advancement and Support of Education (CASE) in Washington, D.C., for their assistance in publishing this book. James L. Fisher, president, and Virginia Carter Smith, vice president, have been very helpful in bringing this publication to life.

A special note of gratitude to Charles Michael Helmken, CASE vice president, for writing the Foreword, and to Robin Goldman, CASE associate editor, for editing, organizing, and improving the manuscript. Thanks to Patricia Allem, D/P Word Processing, for helping to prepare the manuscript. To David W. Barton, Jr., president of The Barton-Gillet Company of Baltimore, Maryland, thanks for allowing me to use an adaptation of "The Communications Process in Marketing" as the basis for the Marketing Model.

Over the years I have been influenced by many conversations, lecturers, symposia, and books. Special thanks to all the people dedicated to improving nonprofit organizations. You, the reader, will find many of their concepts and ideas in the following pages.

Thanks to my grandparents, European immigrants to this country, and to my parents for inspiring in me a love of education and a dedication to learning about nonprofit organizations. This has been supported by my wife, Martha, and my sons, Mark and Brad.

Finally, thanks to you, the reader. I hope you find this publication useful. Take the ideas; apply them, change them, embellish them, adapt them. I wish you and your organization the best of luck.

Dedication

Ronald R. Parent

This publication is dedicated to the memory of Ronald R. Parent (1937-1982), editor and Sibley Award winner for *Notre Dame Magazine*. A native of Maine, Ron joined the Notre Dame publications staff in May 1970, and in both 1978 and 1982 directed the university's magazine to a first-place award among all alumni publications in the nation. The magazine never failed to achieve a Top 10 ranking during Ron's years as editor.

He was a CASE trustee and a frequent participant in CASE conferences and contributor to its publications.

Ron was a journalist in the U.S. Navy from 1957 to 1962 and spent three of those years in Japan. He later attended the University of Maine where he received a journalism degree in 1966. He served as associate editor of *Maine Alumnus* magazine before joining Lafayette College as publications editor. At Notre Dame, Ron completed an M.A. in communications arts in 1974.

Ron's professionalism, creativity, and love for his institution created a model to which others aspire. Unimpressed by his own success, Ron was quick to share his knowledge with others. A high level of quality, respect for his art and craft, quick wit, a sense of humor, and a passion for life characterized Ron. We miss him.

Foreword

Image: an imitation of the external form of a person or thing; a picture, a statue (idol or object of veneration); a counterpart; an exact resemblance; hence an embodiment or type (as "she is the image of purity"); a figure of speech, a simile, a metaphor; a mental picture, as that of a past experience reproduced by memory; an idea; a conception.

Imaging: to picture by one's own mind; to describe or picture effectively by means of language; to represent by a symbol.

—The Winston Dictionary, 1957

I n the beginning, there were images alone, and the earliest humans found ways to create sounds to describe what they saw. And they used charcoal scratches and blood of animals to depict their everyday lives on the walls of caves. That was fairly simple.

Chinese people, early on, created *kanji* picture images to represent not only words but concepts, and other early civilizations used wedge-shaped pictographs on clay and hieroglyphic pictures on stone to create words and tell stories.

They also invented images of their idols and things they could not see or did not wish to reveal. Thus the fish became the Savior and the ship the Church (the first "institutional" image) sailing along on the sea of life. The rock had its great symbolic importance long before Prudential discovered and used it. The Pegasus for the Greeks reigned as the flying horse with superpowers of creativity, and Mobil Oil adopted the animal as its symbol. And so on—with shells and stars, eagles and doves, lions and lambs, crosses, crescents, crests, and crowns.

Then things got more complicated—from images to describe images and words, to words to describe or create images. Letterforms were used to create quasi-images to symbolize establishments and institutions, people and their businesses. From the beginning, colors had maintained their own magic meanings so they could be combined with forms to create more meaningful images.

If I close my eyes, I can conjure my images of my alma mater. The quadrangle at dusk with the shadows cast across the ground by columns of the temples of wisdom, which seemed to have been there since the Greeks; at the foot of the steps to enlightenment, an idol seated on a throne, crowned with laurel, holding high a scepter with a crown on top in her right hand and a left arm gesturing "come and learn." The huge open book in her lap rested below her buxom presence, not nearly as bounteous as the multi-breasted Cybele, hailed in the Middle Ages as alma mater "in signe and token of her grete plente, a grete female ymage," accepted by

German university students as their "beloved mother." I found that Columbia University's goddess was truly a "nourishing mother" for my mind, that the triple crowns on her crest truly symbolized an ancient and noble mission. The pale blue color of her flag, and my graduation hood, confirmed the image that this was a united international community of scholars.

Would that your institution's image could seem to soar like Pegasus, your ship survive a rocky sea filled with fewer fish, your future built on that solid rock supported by many million coins of the realm. Engage in some creative "imaging" to conjure up in your own mind the pictures of your institution that exist in other people's minds. And since pictures are not enough, find the right words to describe the images. Proceed through the pages that follow. You'll find help here for your creative quest.

Charles Michael Helmken
Vice President and Special
  Assistant to the President, CASE
February 1986

Introduction

Any educational institution has an image. That image is not necessarily one concise, cohesive, clear idea. More accurately, an institution's total image consists of many individual sets of perceptions in the minds of its constituents.

Some of these constituents may have had past contact with the institution—for example, alumni, former employees, and donors. Others are presently in contact with the institution; this is the case with students, faculty, administrators, staff, media observers, and competitors. A third set are those who will have future contact, as, for example, faculty, students, staff, administrators, and contributors.

Each of these constituents—past, present, and future—have formed, or will form, an image based on many stimuli. Some of those stimuli come from the institution. Some come from third parties. Others come from the constituents' own imaginations. And still others are passed from person to person.

However they are formed, these people's perceptions are critical to the institution's well-being. How an institution is seen can make the difference between its success and failure. And careful attention to institutional image will reap immediate and long-range rewards.

All signs point to an increasingly competitive future for educational institutions. As competition grows for quality students and faculty, funding, research grants, donations, legislative recognition, alumni support, corporate support, media recognition, and visibility, institutions will become more and more concerned about their images. They will need to maintain distinct positions in the competitive non-profit marketplace, much as corporations strive to achieve and maintain product positions in the competitive for-profit marketplace. And success in the marketplace largely depends on how an institution has been, is, and will be perceived.

What determines image?

Some people think an institution will flourish if it simply "creates a positive image" or "gets national visibility." But image and visibility depend on the institution itself, on its people and activities. You cannot create and maintain a positive image for a poor-quality product. Nor can you maintain a positive image if no substance exists. To market a positive image, you need a product worth marketing. Without that, you are doomed to failure; the efforts and resources would be better spent on improving the product.

What intrinsic characteristics determine the image of an Ivy League university? a Big Ten university? a four-year private institution? a state university? a community college? Think of the names of some institutions. What images do they evoke? Why?

An institution's image comprises many elements. One of the most important of these is leadership. The chancellor or president contributes to (or detracts from) the total institutional image. Because of the leader's high visibility and influence on policy, he or she can significantly influence various audiences' perceptions of the institution.

Faculty are the lifeblood of a college or university. They, too, can positively or negatively influence the institution's image. Those who are reknowned in their fields become spokespersons; observers recognize them and associate them with the institution.

Students also can be a positive or negative force on perceptions of an institution. Student involvement in academics, sports, social events, political affairs, and extracurricular activities contribute to the overall image.

Alumni influence an institution's image. As past graduates go out in the world (and even out of it, as astronauts!), others will see them as representatives of their alma mater.

Inanimate factors contribute toward institutional image, too. How a campus looks, whether buildings are ivy-covered or modern, whether landscaping is neat or down-at-the-heels—all convey an image. Consider how the founders of our country's first colleges and universities approached the architecture of those institutions. Why did many choose a neo-Gothic style? Possibly our educational pioneers were attempting to build on the established image of education in England. They may have hoped to transfer the idea of quality education to the new country through this architectural image.

An institution's programs, of course, also affect the way people perceive it. A university can make deliberate efforts to position itself in viewers' minds by the very courses it offers and by the way it markets those courses.

Most important, though, the image of an educational institution depends upon the quality, scope, and effectiveness of the product it offers: its academic programs. An institution must first be strong in order to be perceived as strong. An institution must *be* what it expects people to perceive it to be.

Still, merely knowing your institution's strengths is not enough; you must communicate those strengths to your constituents. People base their opinions of your institution on their perceptions of it. Those perceptions may not always reflect institutional reality. Thus, you must seek to match people's expectations and perceptions to that reality.

To do this, be sure the image your institution presents reflects what it really is—both its tangible reality, composed of such factors as architecture and course structure, and its intangible reality, composed of leadership, campus atmosphere, and other elements. From the point of view of the external constituent, the image the institution presents will define its reality. You can use that image as a bridge between institutional reality and audience perceptions.

What is quality?

What characteristics can we use to measure and define an institution's quality?

1. *Intrinsic quality and effectiveness of the educational program.* What is the quality of teaching and the educational experience? Is there genuine concern for the educational mission—the very reason the institution exists?

2. *Competence.* Do the institution's faculty, staff, and administrators possess the skill and knowledge necessary to achieve the objectives of its academic mission?

3. *Understanding of consumer needs.* Is the institution truly responsive to client needs? This question applies for every segment of the institution's publics. Do the institution's leaders understand target audiences' demographic characteristics? Have audience needs been considered in the development of the marketing plan?

4. *Reliability.* Is the institution consistent and dependable in its contacts with its constituents?

5. *Credibility.* Is the institution believable? Do claims rest on fact? Are its strengths and weaknesses clear? Does the institution make honest attempts to shore up weak areas? How does it compare to competing institutions?

6. *Access.* Can constituents approach and contact the institution through readily available channels? How easily are complaints resolved?

7. *Security and confidentiality.* Are constituents protected by a secure and trustworthy environment? How are confidential matters handled?

8. *Responsiveness.* Is the institution committed to responding to constituent needs at all levels? How does it express this commitment?

9. *Courtesy.* Are people treated with kindness and courtesy? Are questions answered clearly and easily? How are telephones answered?

10. *Communication.* The essence of marketing is two-way exchange. What communications have been developed? How do they relate to discrete target audiences? How are responses handled? Do outreach materials reflect the institution's true character? Do materials display a sincere attempt to create accurate and honest reader perceptions?

11. *Atmosphere.* In what condition are service facilities, appearance of personnel, buildings, and grounds?

12. *Management and organizational structure.* Is the institution responsive to management? Are administrators carefully chosen? Does the organizational structure support goals and objectives for efficient management? Is the institution's business plan integrated with the academic development plan? Is it integrated with the marketing plan?

13. *Attitudes and self-perception.* What are prevailing feelings of administrators, faculty, staff, and students toward their institution and its people?

Controlling your institution's image

An institution of higher education is alive and ever-changing. It comprises many people, programs, and activities. It is active, not passive—the result of the syn-

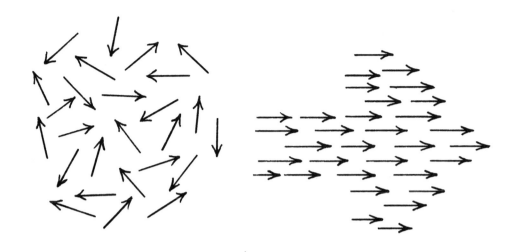

Passive Approach   **Active Approach**

The Passive-Active Approach

ergy that exists as creative people interact. And as an institution changes, its image changes as well.

Many institutions make no effort to direct or control their changing images. This passive approach reflects an institution without comprehensive, coordinated marketing objectives. Actions and events are unrelated; each is an end in itself, designed to reach a specific goal, rather than to contribute to an overall plan. Whatever image exists is accidental, often the result of historical development, location, curricula, special interests, or tradition.

Conversely, in an active approach, image comes about through activities that relate to a unified marketing plan. Institutional actions support each other, and their combined impact contributes to a specific immediate and long-term positive institutional image.

Few institutions have analyzed what their images are, how they got those images, or more important, how the images can be modified or changed. The challenge for educational advancement professionals is to find ways to propagate concise, coordinated institutional images designed to contribute toward planned marketing objectives.

How can you encourage people in your institution to work together to achieve these objectives? You will need creative synergy, the by-product of positive, aggressive management. That, in turn, will let you develop and promote an image effectively.

This book describes ways to identify, develop, and communicate a positive, cohesive image for your institution.

Part I

Identifying Your Institution's Image

Chapter 1

Imagine an Image

How can you describe an image for an educational institution?

An image is the aggregate, or sum, of the feelings, beliefs, attitudes, impressions, thoughts, perceptions, ideas, recollections, conclusions, and mindsets people have of your institution.

Considering this definition, you see that an image is not concrete and precise; it is abstract and complex. Various constituents will probably have different perceptions of your institution. Internal audiences (faculty, staff, students) may have different images of your institution than do external audiences (potential students, parents, alumni, local residents, corporations, foundations). Although these perceptions may have elements in common, an institution's total image is more realistically a collection of many different images.

Your first objective is to create and communicate some positive common image ideas appropriate to all audiences. Another objective is to create and communicate discrete image aspects to discrete target audiences. Think of your institutional image as a central theme with variations on that theme for various audiences. The common aspects are most critical. They will be the ones that position your institution in the marketplace—that is, these aspects will determine the perceived relationship of your institution to its competitors.

What is your image?

How do you determine how your various constituents perceive your institution? Start with market research.

You may decide to hire a professional market research firm. You may use mem-

You may do some of it yourself. Before you decide how to conduct your research, investigate the possibilities.

Before you begin a study, you'll need to answer some questions. What constituent groups do you want to study? Do you want a personal survey, mail survey, telephone survey? You may want to use focus groups—groups of selected individuals who give their impressions in an informal conversational setting. What sample size should you use? What geographic area should you cover? What data collection method is best? What questions should you ask? Many examples of market research exist. Start at your library, with the references listed in the bibliography at the end of this book.

As you determine how people perceive your institution, you must also examine what kind of image your institution projects.

Your institution influences people's perceptions in both tangible and intangible ways. Intangible vehicles include conversations, gossip, word-of-mouth, or any impressions that come from personal contact with your campus and its programs. Tangible vehicles include publications, news stories, transportation vehicles, buildings, signs, films, photographs, or radio and television tapes. Tangible items often create intangible image ideas.

Both tangible and intangible items work separately and in combination to affect your projected image. Consider each item as a stone in a mosaic. Each stone, or item, contains information in itself. More importantly, each contributes to form a larger, more important picture. This is the image your institution projects. That projected image influences your audiences' perceptions of your institution. If the pieces are coordinated, the big picture is clear. If the pieces are uncoordinated, the big picture is muddled, or at worst, incomprehensible.

One way to assess the picture your institution projects is to perform an *image audit*—a review of tangible and intangible items coming from your institution.

Begin by collecting samples of your institution's publications: recruitment brochures, fund-raising pieces, periodicals, newsletters, course booklets, and so on. Lay them out on a table. How do they look together? Do they appear coordinated? What image do they project? Read the copy. How do they describe the institution? How do the descriptions relate? Does each piece of information contribute to your institution's big picture? Review the visuals. Do graphics and photos contribute valuable information? What do these materials communicate individually? collectively? And, finally, how do all these elements relate to the reality of the institution?

Review slide sets, press releases, videotapes, audiotapes, television and radio materials, and other outreach media. Think of the items individually, collectively, and from the point of view of target-audience constituents.

Consider a similar audit of intangible items. What pictures emerge? positive? negative? Most important, are these projected images based on reality?

As you examine your constituents' perceptions and your efforts to influence them, be aware of factors that affect the accuracy of those perceptions. One such factor is time, in the form of *image lag*. Image lag occurs when a person's perceptions of an institution don't keep up with the institution's own changes over

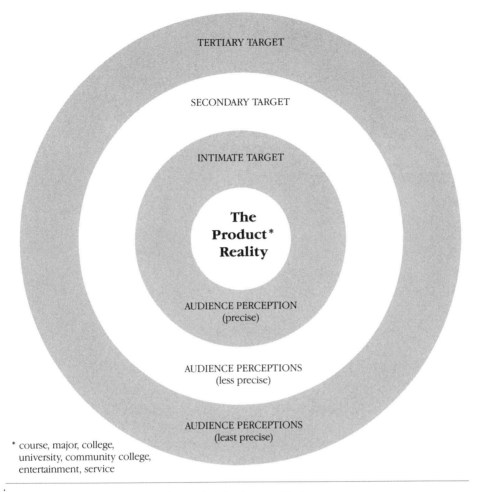

* course, major, college,
  university, community college,
  entertainment, service

Figure 1: The Image Onion

time. In some cases, the lag may be short: recent graduates, local residents, or current students may have fairly accurate, up-to-date images of a college. In other cases, the lag will be longer: a graduate of 25 years ago may have an inaccurate image of a college, based on old perceptions not valid today.

The closeness of a person's contact with your institution can also affect how accurately he or she perceives it. Figure 1 illustrates the *image onion* concept. Perception of a product—the center of the onion—is less precise as one moves farther and farther away from it. This may be affected by geographic distance, frequency of contacts, or quality of information.

Two different theories exist about where image begins. One theory suggests that objective characteristics of an object determine that object's image. The second theory suggests that image depends on the person viewing the object, based on subjective judgments formed by the perceiver.

In fact, both theories are accepted as correct. An institution's image is the result of both objective characteristics of the institution and subjective characteristics of the perceiver, as Figure 2 illustrates.

Keep in mind that a target audience member's objective view of your institu-

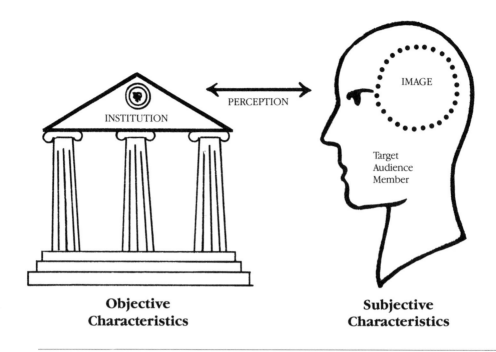

Objective Characteristics

Subjective Characteristics

Figure 2. Objective and Subjective Characteristics

tion may not necessarily reflect his or her subjective attitude. Two members of your target audience may have the same objective view of your institution yet hold very different subjective attitudes about it. For example, two individuals might see Harvard University objectively as a "traditional" or "conservative" institution. However, their attitudes might differ; one person might consider a "traditional" institution to be high-quality or prestigious, while the other might think of it as boring or constraining. Thus, although Harvard's objective characteristics remain the same, the two people will hold different total images of the university.

Grasping the global image

Figure 3 depicts an educational institution. The institution comprises majors, departments, and colleges. It has many target audiences. Each audience group, and each individual audience member, may perceive the institution and its components differently. Several factors will influence these perceptions: the institution's outreach efforts; outside sources (external influences); and, most important, the reality of the institution itself.

In addition, groups and individuals affect other groups and individuals with a synergistic influence called image link. The total environment is always changing. New influences and ideas constantly affect image perceptions. In turn, your institutional image—and those of your competitors—are changing as well. You must constantly be aware of both your institution's image and its position in the competitive marketplace.

The collective image of your institution, or *global institutional image*, is the total of many audience members' perceptions. This global image should contain some recurring components, the key ideas you want to communicate to each target audience. An institution cannot change images as an actor changes costumes to play different roles. The institution can, however, project image variations that have common key ideas. These variations allow you to develop and deliver custom information to each target audience. The key ideas, as the common threads binding your global image into a cohesive whole, will help position your institution in relation to others in the competitive marketplace.

Corporate marketers know that it is differences, not similarities, that distinguish products. Educational institutions, as well, must be sensitive to product differentiation. Think of your educational majors, courses, and programs as products. Product differentiation can occur at a broad level (institution to institution) or at a more precise level (among departments, majors, courses, or other offerings).

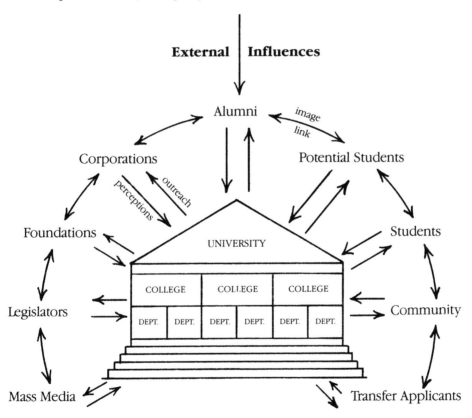

An educational institution, its publics, and how it's perceived.

Figure 3: Global Institutional Image

In summary, you should consider the following points in examining your institution's image:

1. Decide what market research should be done to measure your institution's image, and who should do it.

2. Audit tangible and intangible outreach materials.

3. Examine the potential image lag for each constituency.

4. Determine how various audiences perceive your institution, and why.

5. Describe your global institutional image.

6. Develop key image ideas.

7. Look at your position in the competitive market. How does your image affect your institution's position?

Chapter 2

Everything About An Institution "Talks"

Think of your target audience member's mind as a computer. The computer can input, store, classify, search for, and retrieve bits of information about your institution. New information put into storage can change old information. New information can replace old information. New information can reclassify old information. The bits of information, when looked at collectively, form the person's total image of your institution. A new "print-out" will display the most current information, or image.

Your responsibility is to identify the "computers" that are most important (define target audiences), assess the computer state-of-mind (conduct market research), provide new input as necessary (communicate), and reassess the computer memory (do follow-up research).

As this metaphor suggests, images are not static. New perceptions—or adjustments of old perceptions—can change images. A member of your target audience forms perceptions of your institution and its components as a result of many stimuli, tangible and intangible. Some may be accurate; others may not be.

Some stimuli that contribute to your institution's image may be out of your control. You cannot, for instance, control external sources—such as information passed in conversation. Similarly, you probably cannot control many aspects of your product, although your market research may provide a basis for proposing changes. Each institution must consider a balance between market-driven services and institutional missions and objectives.

Some of the information your institution produces is *formal:* the annual report, speeches from the chief executive officer, press releases, catalogs, mailers, radio advertisements, signs, letters, and direct mail. Other information is *informal:* an alumnus speaking to a potential student, a letter to the editor in your alumni magazine, a student notice on a bulletin board, a newspaper editorial. Some of the information is *factual:* the location, size, type of institution, current clientele. Some is *qualitative* information on the quality of the curriculum and its relevance to the consumer. Image is created by formal, informal, factual, and qualitative stimuli.

For the most part, you cannot control informal information about your institution. You can, of course, try to change negative perceptions. For example, by responding to an editorial that presented misinformation, you can hope to change some perceptions by providing correct data. Remember, the "computer" mind is flexible. However, communication research indicates it's easier to create opinions where none exist than it is to *change* opinions, once formed. The "computer" mind will accept new information that replaces old information only if the new information is truthful and logical.

Although you can try to counteract negative images that come from informal sources, in the long run it is much more effective to focus on the cause than merely to treat the symptoms. Your institution can indirectly encourage informal sources to disseminate positive information by creating a positive image among those sources themselves—students, faculty, alumni, administrators, and staff. If these people are happy with the institution, they'll say so. Such word-of-mouth communication can be your institution's most powerful image-building tool.

Remember, though, that your institution's informal sources will be the people most closely connected with its daily operations. They will base their own opinions of the institution on their personal experiences. Thus, as I explained earlier, the image your institution presents must be based on reality. If it isn't, it will conflict with what your internal constituents know to be true. No image program will succeed if perceptions do not match reality.

Everything counts

Many institutional communicators tend to think narrowly. For instance, they may consider the college alumni magazine only in terms of its primary function: communicating with past graduates. They may give little thought to how that magazine contributes to perceptions and images of a different audience—potential students. These communicators should consider potential students and their parents as a major secondary audience.

Similarly, communicators have traditionally tended to think of a fund-raising direct mail piece in terms of its ability to raise money, without considering its implications for related objectives. Yet in higher education, fund raising must support alumni work, alumni work must support fund raising and student recruitment—and so on. Successful institutions research, plan, deliver, and evaluate outreach materials that all contribute to a particular global institutional identity. Each effort supports other efforts; this process creates a collective strength.

Everything about an institution talks. Everything communicates. The institution's programs, its administration, faculty, students, and alumni "speak" about the institution. Items that may at first seem hardly significant still contribute to the institution's image. These include every document, speech, sign, label, envelope, letterhead, certificate, photograph, television image, postcard, illustration, newspaper article, calling card, bus, truck, map, poster, conversation, rubber stamp, indicia, notebook cover, bookstore knick-knack, printed placemat, radio advertisement, mission statement, board member's occupation, telephone operator's tone of voice, fund-raising letter, logo, security vehicle, hand-written note—all contribute to an institution's image.

Consider a book in terms of levels of stimuli. At a very basic level, a book can be perceived as a three-dimensional object made of paper, with shape, texture, color, and size. At a higher level, a book can be considered an information storage device. It can be seen in terms of information retrieval (reading). At an even higher level, a book can be considered in relation to other books (say, within a library). At this level, the book becomes part of a larger, more theoretical system.

Consider your institution in terms of levels of stimuli. For example, think of your admissions search mailer. At the most basic level, the mailer is a document that contains editorial and photographic information written and designed to attract students. At the highest level, the search mailer is a sophisticated stimulus perceived in context with other stimuli and measured with and against information stored in the reader's mind. Depending upon the receiver, the mailer can affect perceptions in such areas as development, continuing education, placement, sponsored research, alumni, community affairs, and sports events.

What are your "talkers" saying?

Once they decide to improve the way their institutions are perceived, unsophisticated marketers tend to react by producing materials that all look the same and say almost the same thing. For some institutions, this may be a good approach. A small school or college may be able to develop and project a tightly coordinated image. (After all, isn't much of Coca-Cola's® success related to the fact that the company produces and markets each of its products with a distinct package, color, and logo?)

But for other institutions, such factors as size, structure, or internal politics make an imposed common image impractical. In these cases, the marketer may think of an overall common denominator with a separate, but related, identity for each component. For a large institution, the institution's name may serve as that common denominator. Each major component may have a separate identity under the generic "umbrella" or institutional image of the parent organization. A corporate example is General Motors Corporation.® The parent identifier is GMC.® Chevrolet,® Pontiac,® and Cadillac® are examples of subunit entities with separate but related identities.

The approach you should take depends on such factors as the political climate at your institution. How tightly coordinated do you want your institution's components to be? What is possible? What will be best for the future? Choose your course carefully.

At first, the idea of creating a planned positive image for your institution may seem an impossible task. But it isn't. Let's examine some ideas that can help you get the job done.

I recall my college art professor asking us one day what we had seen on our way to drawing class. My classmates and I looked at each other with blank astonishment. We had seen nothing. Nothing unusual. No automobile accidents. No special events. Nothing.

The lecture that day was about perception. Of course we had "seen" something—many things, all sorts of stimuli. Visual images. Sounds. Actions. People. Colors. Things. The world around us was alive with stimuli. At every moment our senses were bombarded with input that added to, modified, or changed our perceptions of things around us.

The same is true of your institution. Stimuli abound.

Review your course catalog. What curricula does it describe? How are majors, departments, and colleges structured? What images do different courses communicate? Individually? Collectively?

Spend some time in your mailroom. Review your institution's outreach materials. What do they say—individually and collectively? To whom? Why?

Read your institution's newspaper. Read student publications, questionnaire responses, official publications. Read press clippings about your institution. What are individual and collective messages?

Walk through your bookstore or gift shop. What's being communicated? Listen to conversations in your dining hall. What are people saying? Why? Look at architecture, interior decoration, signs, posters, displays, vehicles. What collective image do they project?

Call your institution. How are the phones answered? How is your institution listed in the telephone directory?

Ask your neighbors about your institution. How do they feel about it? Do they see it as an asset to the community?

Students are excellent sources of information. Ask a freshman about his or her reaction to your admissions process. Attend a high school college night where your admissions staff presents its wares. Watch audience reactions. Note questions. What handouts do people select? Why?

To understand and improve your institution's image, you need to look in two directions—inward and outward. Spend some time examining internal materials and information, all the things that "talk" about your institution. Each item, individually and collectively, contributes to the institutional image.

Outward, or external, examination requires that you focus on various target audiences. What are their perceptions? Do these perceptions reflect reality? What needs to be done to change perceptions? How is your institution and its components perceived in relation to competing institutions? Media relations, community relations, and other outreach activities as well as internal communications play an important role in image development. These activities should be carefully monitored and controlled to assure they contribute to the institution's image.

Higher education's product is education. The process of research, teaching, and learning forms the core of every institution. And, like other products, education has its variations. Some institutions excel in undergraduate education in certain disciplines; others focus on vocational education; some are noted for graduate education; some are educational "halfway houses" preparing students for advanced education; some specialize in research. Higher education is not monolithic. Every institution offers different products and different product mixes. What are yours? How do they relate to the competition? How do they contribute toward your image?

In summary:

1. How do your key target audiences perceive your institution? How must you change those images?

2. What image(s) do your institution's formal communications project? Individually? Collectively?

3. How can your institution develop a global institutional identity?

4. What type of image should your institution consider? tight? or an umbrella image with separate component identities?

Chapter 3

What's in a Name?

Most institutional advancement people take their institutions' names for granted. But an institution's name is the first thing that sets it apart from competing institutions. The name is the identifier. It communicates identity. It contributes to an institution's image.

Would a rose by any other name smell as sweet?

Would John Wayne have earned cinema reputation if he had used his real name (Marion Morrison)?

Would Chicago plumber George Holmes have experienced a 600 percent increase in business in his predominately Polish neighborhood if he had not changed his business name to "Dombrowski and Holmes"?

An English teacher in Sugar Grove, Illinois, queries his classes, "What do you think tomorrow's substitute teacher, Bertha Smith, will be like?" The students universally think she will be old, fat, and probably mean. When asked what they think their substitute teacher named Stephanie Smith will be like, they say she's young and beautiful (and all the boys say they'll sit up front that day).

Some African tribes whisper secret names in babies' ears to give them a good start in life. Throughout history names with power have ranged from the Aztec Texcatlipoca to the fairy tale Rumplestiltskin.[1]

Major corporations hire consultants to help come up with names for products or for the corporations themselves. That's how Cities Service Corporation became Citgo. International marketing often brings problems as words from one language are translated into another. Kavli,® the trade name for a Norwegian fish roe paste, brings smiles in Greece, where the word means "sexually aroused." Coca-Cola,® in China, translates into either "wax-fattened mare" or "bite the wax tadpole" depending on how it's pronounced. Names communicate!

What does your institution's name say?

Many institutional names provide more than identity. Some communicate location: Syracuse University, Ithaca College, El Paso Community College, Worcester Academy, or the University of Portland. Others are named after individuals: Cornell University, Harvey Mudd College, Lafayette College, Brigham Young University, or Baruch College. Other names suggest activities: Air Force Military Academy, Rhode Island School of Design (a combination of location and activity), or the John Jay College of Criminal Justice (a combination of name and activity). Some names have evolved from religious ideas: University of Notre Dame, Immaculata College, Rosary College, or Yeshiva University.

Higher education comprises many kinds of institutions—preparatory schools, technical schools, community colleges, private colleges, public colleges, four-year private universities, and four-year public (state-supported) universities. Often words describing the kind of institution appear in the name: Washburn University, Asbury College, Bemidji State University, Berkeley Preparatory School, Charles County Community College, or the Delaware Technical and Community College.

Names communicate ideas as well. Market research shows that the name Cornell University evokes ideas of quality, research, and location ("far above Cayuga's waters"). Market research might disclose some useful ideas for building on your institution's name.

A name that communicates positive ideas is an asset. Others sometimes confuse external audiences. Consider the dilemma of Washington University, which is located not in the District of Columbia nor in the state of Washington but rather in St. Louis, Missouri! Its board of trustees has stipulated that the institution add "of St. Louis" to the university's name every time it's identified.

Other confusing names include Indiana University of Pennsylvania, California State College of Pennsylvania, Citrus College (Florida or California?), College of the Desert (Arizona, New Mexico, California?), College of Notre Dame (located in Belmont, California, but which might be confused with the university in Indiana), and National University (which could be anywhere in the country!).

A name that is the same as or similar to other institutions' names can also cause confusion. Think about these seven educational institutions: Westminster Choir College (New Jersey), Westminster College (Missouri), Westminster College (Pennsylvania), Westminster College (Utah), Westminster School (Connecticut), the Westminster Schools (Georgia), and Westminster Theological Seminary (Pennsylvania).

Acronyms spread like weeds in nonprofit fields. Some educational institutions have been successful in identifying themselves using acronyms: UCLA, NYU, MIT, and RPI, for example. But acronyms can be a source of confusion as well. Before you begin to use an acronym as an identifier for your institution, consider two things: First, is your acronym unique, or do others use the same acronym? (OSU can identify Ohio State University or Oklahoma State University.) Second, where are your target audiences? How will they perceive your acronym? (OSU may clearly identify Ohio State University to people in Columbus, Ohio. How will it be interpreted in Oklahoma City?)

Think about your institution's name from an external audience member's point-of-view. What information does it communicate? Is it positive? Does it help clarify the institution? Or is it confusing?

Make the most of your name

Most institutions do not want to change their names. If your institution's name is confusing to external audiences, you may want to consider adding a clarifier. Clarifiers—descriptive words or phrases added to the name—can help position the institution in the competitive marketplace. For example:

Institution's name	Institution's name with added clarifier
Mission College	*Mission College,* of La Jolla, California
Western University	*Western University,* a four-year publicly supported institution in Boise, Idaho
Madison Medical School	*Madison Medical School,* specializing in ophthalmology
Atlantic State University	*Atlantic State University,* state-supported, nonresidential, exciting
Immaculate Conception College	*Immaculate Conception College,* a four-year Roman Catholic college for theological study

Changing or modifying an institution's name can be a subtractive process. Adding clarifiers is an additive process and is very flexible. Clarifiers need not be permanent; they can change as the institution changes. An institution may want to consider developing different clarifiers for different target audiences.

For example, imagine a large mythical educational institution, ABC University. Here are some examples of clarifiers that could be used for discrete university target audiences:

Target Audience	Clarifier
Undergraduate admissions	*ABC University* Quality education in the heart of New York City.

Graduate admissions	*ABC University* Quality graduate education. New York City with its many resources is our campus.
Transfer admissions	*ABC University* Educational opportunities in many fields of study.
Development	*ABC University* A multidisciplinary university in an urban setting.
Alumni	*ABC University* Tradition combined with contemporary education.
Community affairs	*ABC University* A university with a commitment to the city.

The power of a name

To you, your institution's name is a familiar symbol of a well-understood list of activities. To outside constituents, however, the name is merely one among many. In response to certain cues, specific names will emerge ahead of others in the listener's mind. This process is called associative memory.

To visualize how associative memory works, imagine yourself surrounded by thousands of television sets all playing at once. There are groups of television sets for every type of educational institution. Think of one type—say, private universities. Your mind will focus on one bank of television sets blaring out a cacophony of sound and many colorful visuals. After a moment you notice only one set—for you, perhaps it will be the one representing Harvard University. Your attention centers on Harvard; the others blend together in the background.

Associative memory is automatic. It happens every time you need selective information. Because of associative memory, Harvard University takes priority, for some listeners, among the generic group of images called "private universities."

Associative memory works in reverse as well. A name alone will evoke, first, an image of that institution. But the listener's associative memory may in turn link that name to a large class of institutions. Thus, the name "Harvard University" has both a denotative function and a connotative function. All names both connote and denote concepts. These concepts are evoked when a name is recalled.

Names that contain valuable information achieve priority positions in the recaller's mind. The more meaningful the name, the more powerful it is, and the easier for the mind to recall it. In the corporate world of vitamins, for instance, the name One-A-Day® will be easier to recall than Theragran-M.®

A name can contain many coding cues, or points of association. A listener may code an abstract word like "health" both as language (phonetically) or as a concept (semantically). More precise terms like "aerobic exercise" can be coded phonetically, semantically, physically, or emotionally.

Marketing by name

Commercial product marketers know two important factors of product success in the marketplace: identity and repetition.

They realize, for instance, that the average supermarket has more than 10,000 products on the shelves. They seek to create an identity for each product to differentiate it from the rest. Educational institutions also offer many products. An institution should build its image on the factors that make its product different: the type of education it offers, location, facilities, the quality of educational programs, faculty, athletics, faculty-to-student ratios, kinds of students it accepts. The marketer must weigh each factor carefully and mix it into the image recipe. The marketer must then encourage the audience to connect that image with the institution's name.

The Mississippi University for Women faced a marketing dilemma when its name ceased to reflect its identity. The state's Supreme Court mandated that the university accept men. The board of trustees and some of the administrators wanted to continue calling their institution a university for women. They argued that this had been their focus for many decades and they did not want to change. Should the name continue as the Mississippi University for Women? Or should it be changed? The dilemma continues unresolved despite a growing number of male students.

Institutions have many levels of identity. A large university, for example, has a name; in addition, its colleges have names, departments have names, and academic majors have names. Each cries out for identity. Although you may not be able to change the name of your parent institution, you may have opportunities to develop names for subunits or for individual activities. Remember the importance of identifying each subunit in relation to the parent institution.

As you maintain appropriate identity at each level, be careful that one level does not gain identity at the expense of another. How many departmental letterheads have you seen which pay little or no homage to the parent institution? Each subunit should be identified in relation to the hierarchical structure of the institution. This idea can be communicated through appropriate type size and placement. Again, when preparing outreach materials, imagine how they will be perceived externally.

Internal political issues may contribute to confusion about hierarchical identity. For many years I worked in the public relations office at the University of Rochester. Typical of similar private institutions, the university comprised many schools and colleges. Most units (the Memorial Art Gallery, the College of Medicine and Dentistry, the College of Business Administration) had no problem of identity in relation to the parent institution. However, the Eastman School of Music, a component with a highly regarded international reputation, constantly sought individual identity. Should identity be maintained as The Eastman School of Music, The Eastman School of Music of the University of Rochester, or the University of Rochester Eastman School of Music? This may seem a trivial concern, but imagine the confusion it creates for external audiences.

Once an institution determines its identity, it must establish that identity with repetition through the various media.

Many advancement professionals miss opportunities to identify their institution. It's amazing to see press releases that do not include any reference to the institution. You should build into every news story information that will help to position the institution. Similarly, many institutional publications do not include clear statements of identity—often the name appears only in a return mailing address or buried in body copy. Examine critically all outreach materials—publications, press releases, PSA's, speeches, calling cards, letterheads—from the receiver's viewpoint. Is each piece well-identified? Does it add information that will help the receiver understand your institution? How does it help to position your institution in the competitive marketplace?

Follow the lead of corporations, which are careful to identify their products, their transportation vehicles, all printed materials, and even, in some cases, their employees (with uniforms). Find and use every opportunity to identify your institution by name.

Some institutional advancement professionals complain that their institution's name is "a word no one has ever heard of." Remember, once Kodak® and Xerox® were words no one had ever heard of. George Eastman, founder of Eastman Kodak Corporation, invented "Kodak." The word "Xerox" was created by a computer!

To successfully market your institution you must:

1. Understand its name. What images does the name evoke? What are its limitations and opportunities?

2. Consider adding clarifiers to your institution's name. Will additional information help target audiences better understand your services and activities?

3. Understand the hierarchical structure of your institution. What are the subunits? How are they identified? How can each maintain separate identity while contributing to the parent institution's identity?

4. Remember the image building formula: identity plus repetition equals success. Take every opportunity to identify your institution.

---

[1] Charles Leroux, "For some, a rose by any name is still thorny," *Chicago Tribune*, Oct. 2, 1983, p. D-3.

Part II

Creating an Image Program

Chapter 4

Who Builds an Image?

A n educational institution must focus attention on the people who create and maintain its image. Marketing techniques, materials, and plans do not by themselves produce successful institutional image programs. People do. You need the skills, support, and agreement of a coordinated team.

In the corporate world, many people contribute to developing a company's identity. The chief executive officer, board of directors, vice presidents, marketing director, sales director, advertising manager, and other key leaders help decide on a corporate image. The corporation then implements an image program involving as many channels as possible: mission statements, product development, sales approaches, graphic standard manuals, advertising strategies, public relations, and outreach efforts. All areas of the company's operation contribute to building a cohesive, coordinated image. The process involves many people doing many things.

Likewise, educational institutions should involve many people in developing institutional identity. The board of trustees, president, faculty, alumni, students, and staff all play roles. The challenge is to combine information from these many sources into a concise, coherent image.

An educational institution is a complex community. Its strength may lie in the fact that it harbours diverse opinions. Such a strength may prove a weakness, though, when it comes to image development. Often an institution holds so many lines of authority and power that creating and projecting a comprehensive image may seem impossible.

Forming an image team

An educational institution contemplating a comprehensive effort to identify, plan, and implement an image program should first examine the people who will be involved. Are staff members with the appropriate skills available to carry out a comprehensive image program? If not, you may need outside help.

Some institutions hire professional firms to research, plan, develop, and maintain cohesive image programs. This approach has some advantages—it brings to the institution outsiders who aren't biased by past events or internal political pressures. Decisions can be impersonal and objective. But firms vary in quality and knowledge. And they can be expensive. You should not, however, discount using consultants—especially if you do not have the necessary skills in-house. (In its membership directory, CASE lists some commercial organizations that provide various image development services to educational institutions.)

Your institution may be fortunate in identifying the necessary skills among your administrators, faculty, staff, or advisory board members. The next requirement is an environment that supports image development. People must want to work together. Perhaps your president, key faculty members, administrators, or respected board members can encourage this. Image plans created in isolation will probably fail, as will mandated plans, imposed by a few on the many.

Those in charge must keep the needs of subunits in mind as they draw up objectives. How would a comprehensive image and marketing plan for a community college help the departments of computer science or physical education? help individual faculty members? help students? How could an improved image for the mathematics department help the total image of the college? The image makers must seek creative ideas from people throughout the institution.

Start with marketing

What skills do you need to identify, plan, create, and deliver a comprehensive institutional image? The most important skill is marketing—or, more precisely, an understanding of marketing concepts as they relate to educational institutions.

Marketing skills include knowledge of market research techniques, market planning, audience segmentation, demographics, image analysis, persuasion, communications, and media placement. Your image team as a whole must understand the concept of product differentiation. Image creation begins with identifying your institutional product and recognizing its advantages over competitors' products. This produces *comparative differential advantage* for your product in the eyes of the consumer.

Some people argue that marketing and development are superfluous to the basic mission of a nonprofit institution. The successful marketer should not overlook these objections. Rather, he or she should listen carefully to these arguments and work cautiously to change attitudes. Marketing educational institutions often requires that the marketer first become an educator.

Institutions cannot and should not simply pluck successful marketing people from the corporate world and expect them to succeed automatically in the nonprofit sector. Educational institutions have separate sets of values, ethics, traditions, objectives, and *raisons d'être.* Before a marketing professional can succeed in this environment, he or she must first thoroughly understand it.

Political hierarchy can vary from one institution to another. At one institution the board of trustees and the president may hold political power. At another, which, for instance, is engaged heavily in research, the faculty may hold the reins. It would be difficult, if not impossible, to find similar ranges of organizational power structure in the corporate world.

Institutional marketing people must realize they are working in atypical, and often delicate, environments. They must realize that an institution has evolved, sometimes over centuries, to its current state. Most educational institutions are ruled by consensus. Ideas that are not clearly understood and accepted will not work. Marketers must demonstrate a special sensitivity to and compassion for their institutions' traditions, missions, and objectives. And their motives must clearly support advancement of the institution.

Who do you need?

Marketing alone does not produce successful institutional image programs. Your team must represent skills in research, planning, publications, media support, strategies, and evaluation.

One vital skill is creative writing. A creative writer communicates the nature of an institution to target audiences.

A good creative writer is difficult to find. The writer needs to understand the institution thoroughly and be able to identify its advantages. The writer must begin with intimate knowledge of the institution's mission, curriculum, strengths, and weaknesses. He or she must also be familiar with competing institutions in order to position his or her own institution in the marketplace.

Bad writing is dull, boring, and static. Good writing is exciting, interesting, and active. It requires imagination, creativity, understanding, dedication, and a love for the language. The best writers are passionate about their work. They use words, sentences, and paragraphs as tools to create pictures in the reader's mind. They challenge and stimulate. They weave beautiful tapestries.

Institutional writing comes in many forms—catalogs, direct mail pieces, letters, speeches, news, promotions, feature articles, and so on. Far too many institutions distribute publications filled with mediocre, uninspired, boring writing. A well-written news release can add powerful information to your institutional image. Likewise, a feature story can contribute positive impressions. Direct mail, a special writing art in itself, can offer pleasant reading, help position the institution, motivate the reader, and achieve results.

The best writing appeals to the reader's mind, intellect, and soul. It links the institution, its marketing purpose, and the reader. It helps to set that institution apart from competing institutions.

In addition to the writers themselves, your image team needs editors to work with what others have written. Don't confuse an editor with a creative writer. Their skills are different, and both play important roles in developing good publications.

Quality writing, well edited, deserves quality design. The creative designer combines color, shape, typography, format, illustration, texture, and layout in the same way the writer combines words. He or she must create communications pieces that stand individually while conveying additional visual information to the target audiences.

Your graphic imagery program must combine consistency and flexibility. Consistent features provide continuity; flexibility allows presentation of new and different information. The design program must have room to grow, develop, and change as the institution and its components change.

There is a tendency, especially on the part of individuals who do not understand creative design, to think that every outreach piece should look the same. How effective would McDonald's® advertising campaigns be if each ad looked the same? The key idea is unity *plus* multiplicity. There should be some common threads in each piece so that the target audience member will associate each new piece with his or her current image of the institution. Each piece should be a thread contributing to the larger institutional fabric.

Ideally, the writer and designer will spark ideas in each other. The best publications come from writers, editors, designers, and photographers who understand marketing, work well together, and can contribute their skills to achieving a common objective.

Other visual media can advance your institutional image program. In fact, research shows our society is becoming more and more visual. Visual media, such as photography, television, and illustration, can help translate your institution to target audiences.

Visual images are powerful tools. They can sum up complex ideas. They can have impact and permanence. Build a library of visual images in videotape, color photographs, and black-and-white photographs. Consider each visual image as one more stone that can add information to the mosaic of collective institutional image.

One often-overlooked skill, distribution, can make the difference between success and failure for your program. Lists of media outlets, target audiences, and other constituents must be kept up-to-date. The most carefully prepared image campaign will fail if it does not reach the right audience or is diluted because it misses its most appropriate targets.

As educational institutions move from passive to active marketing and image development, we must reappraise staff roles, skills, and abilities. Writers and editors, who in the past were valued only in terms of "passive" copy editing, now play an important role in the success of their institution. Designers, who were considered only as producers of camera-ready mechanicals, can contribute vital skills to image development. Photographers, who were thought handy only for passport and "grip-and-grin" photos, can now add their visual skills. Public relations staff, who were seen useful only to announce events, can exercise marketing skills to support the institution and its components. A new age has dawned!

To successfully build your institution's image you must:

1. Identify the image building team. Who should be involved? Should you consider external commercial services?

2. Identify the skills necessary to develop your institution's image. Are those skills available on campus? Should you plan to purchase skills from outside sources?

3. Review written materials. Measure writing in relation to image objectives. Do the same for design, photography, and other visual media.

4. Decide how an effective image building team could be put together. Who will do what, and why?

Chapter 5

Global Institutional Marketing: Synergy in Action

For many educational institutions, change occurs very slowly. This is both an asset and a liability. It is an asset when an institution does not respond to every whim, trend, and fad that comes along. It's a liability if, when new ideas do appear, they are overlooked or adopted much too slowly.

Marketing and image building, new ideas for educational institutions, may meet resistance in the academic world. For the concepts to be most effectively implemented, some traditional ways of doing things have to be changed.

This chapter is dedicated to the idea of change—change to achieve better results, not change for change's sake alone.

Creating a global marketing program

One common problem in implementing institutional marketing and image development programs stems from the ways institutions are traditionally organized. Most institutions have distinct vertical components. Marketing and image development activities can occur in many of these components. For example, a university may comprise several colleges, and each college may have its own programs for admissions, development, promotion, community relations, and media relations. Because of the institution's vertical organization, few administrative positions cut horizontally across the institution. As a result, it is difficult to implement a strong, institution-wide marketing and image program.

A college or university needs a coordinated *horizontal* marketing system to advance itself and create a positive image in the minds of constituents. The effort must cut across traditional boundaries in order to succeed. I call such an effort *global institutional marketing.*

How can an institution achieve global institutional marketing?

One way would be to create an administrative position that cuts across traditional vertical boundaries. The person in this position needs administrative authority and the power to take a broad-view approach to marketing and advancement activities. The person's capabilities should include marketing, promotion, advertising, public relations, and institutional advancement. Most important is the person's commitment to the institution. "Marketers" plucked from the corporate sector, with little or no background or sensitivity for their institution, may exacerbate problems rather than solve them, as I discussed in the last chapter.

Another way to implement global institutional marketing is to create a task force of people from both inside and outside the institution. Such a task force of staff members, faculty, students, board members, and alumni could direct global institutional marketing efforts for a college or university. The task force must have the authority to implement ideas. The team should be chosen carefully and fairly. Its success depends, to a great degree, on how others at the institution perceive it—that is, on its own image.

The global institutional marketing director or task force should seek to initiate, maintain, and monitor activities in research, planning and strategy, outreach, and evaluation. Support from top management and from the board of directors or trustees is critical. It's vital that the director or task force members know the institution, understand how to work with people, and be willing to work hard.

Benefits of a global marketing program

Remember, your global institutional image—that is, your institution's total image—is really an aggregate of many images, a collection of perceptions in the minds of the many people who come into contact with your institution. Your institution's target audiences are *not* separate, distinct entities; they overlap. An individual may end up forming perceptions of your institution based on stimuli from many areas of the institution.

Without a coordinated marketing program, various components of an institution will often produce unrelated messages, or even conflicting ones. This, in turn, can create a confused, fragmented image in the minds of the people perceiving the institution.

A global marketing program, however, allows you to build a coordinated, multilevel image structure for your institution (see figure 4). In higher education, the university or college image serves as an "umbrella" covering its various components, each of which has its own image and enjoys its own identity. Outreach efforts for a component must consider implications for other components that share target audience members. Each component's efforts, instead of conflicting with those of other components, can support them.

A global outlook helps a school, college, or university monitor institutional and component images as presented in all outreach materials. All the things that talk about the institution—publications, media coverage, the CEO's image—should

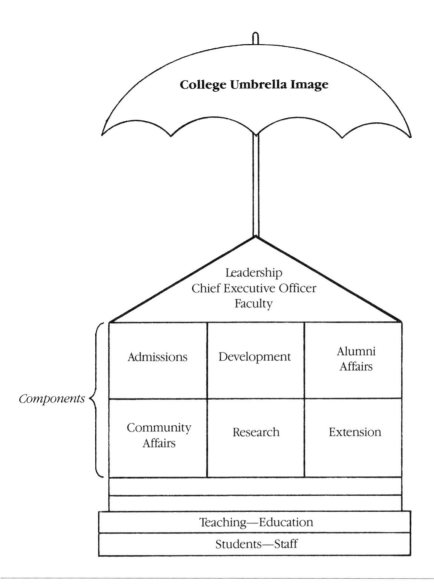

Figure 4: Institutional and Component Images

reflect a cohesive image for your institution and its components.

In summary:

1. How can you cut across traditional vertical boundaries with coordinated marketing and image-building efforts?

2. Should your institution create a position or appoint a task force to implement global institutional marketing?

3. How does your institutional image plan relate to discrete target audiences?

4. How can you combine a generic, institution-wide, global image with images of individual components?

Chapter 6

How to Build an Image

Art historians like to tell a story of the Renaissance sculptor Michelangelo Buonarroti. An admirer was impressed by the famous artist's powerful, provocative, life-like sculptures. They seemed more human than stone. The admirer asked Michelangelo how he did it. According to the tale, Michelangelo replied, "It's really not that difficult. I start with a large block of Carrara marble and just take away all the stone that's unnecessary."

Creating an institutional image should be done in just the opposite way—by adding, not subtracting. Institutional advancement people "just" need to understand their institution, research, plan, and do everything else necessary, for the right audiences, with the right materials, the right timing, and the right distribution. Of course it takes the skills of many Michelangelos to do this. Creativity, imagination, dedication, and perseverance will help create a planned institutional image and communicate it to target audiences.

Let's examine ways to create a positive image for an institution using the additive process. The steps are:

I.   Use research to measure target audience image perceptions and attitudes.

II.   Understand your institution.

III.   Establish comparative differential advantage.

IV.   Make and carry out an image/marketing plan, involving many people as you go.

V.   Measure, evaluate, and maintain your image, and refine your image program as necessary.

Step I: Use research to measure your current image

In Chapter 1, I discussed the importance of research. You need information about your target audience's perceptions of the total institution. You also need information about how various audiences perceive the institution's individual components.

Research can be complex and confusing. It is, however, an important cornerstone upon which you should build your image program. Effective research will also provide valuable information about competing institutions. Research will help you visualize your institution, its programs, and its activities as your target audiences see them in relation to your competitors.

Institutions have been using research for a long time. Admissions staffs use data from the Educational Testing Service; the American College Testing Service; and other local, state, and national services. Development offices use alumni surveys, feasibility studies, and computerized data on alumni and donors. Some institutions conduct attitude studies with various target audiences. Often, however, these departments do not share their results or even find ways to use findings to achieve their objectives. They conduct research only to answer specific queries or to help carry out specific tasks. For maximum results in developing a comprehensive image, you need access to all this information, and you need to develop ways to apply it effectively.

What research techniques can you use to measure target audience perceptions?

• *Focus groups* consist of pre-selected representatives of a target audience, usually eight to 12 people, led through discussion in an informal setting. A leader asks the group to respond to predetermined research topics. Often the one- to two-hour session is audiotaped or videotaped. In the corporate world, researchers use basic information from focus groups to plan more comprehensive research. You can use focus groups for this or for gathering broad, general information. Because the members of a focus group may not be representative of the larger audience, be careful not to put too much stock in their views. They give clues, not evidence, of the target audience's opinions.

• *Mail surveys* use written questionnaires to gather specific information. One advantage of a mail survey is its comparatively low cost: it's an economical way to reach many people at many locations. A disadvantage is the generally low response rate. Response depends on such factors as timing, the respondent's interest in or relationship to the surveyor, or incentives (you may wish to include an incentive item such as a college decal, events or sports schedule, or ticket discount coupon).

To be valid, mail surveys require special skills and knowledge on the surveyor's part. You must create questionnaires carefully; such factors as word choice or question sequence can influence the way the reader interprets and responds to the questions. You will need to test the survey instrument on a small sample representing your target audience. You may want to follow up with personal interviews or phone interviews. Assess your in-house capabilities carefully before launching a full-scale mail survey.

• *Telephone surveys* have the advantage of selectivity. Mail surveys may be answered by someone other than the target audience member; with a telephone survey, you have more control over who responds. These surveys also require careful preparation, especially in question sequence. Usually, the survey "builds" from general to specific and from easy to difficult, so you can gather as much information as possible without alienating the respondent.

A disadvantage with telephone surveys is time; most are limited to five or 10 minutes. They also require a great deal of labor. You must train your interviewers; don't assume you can turn this duty over to inexperienced volunteers. Again, consider your capabilities carefully before beginning.

• *Direct intercept research* involves surveyors approaching and questioning people at a specific location. This is also called "mall intercept research," since consumer studies often use shopping malls as survey sites. Like telephone and mail surveys, intercept surveys use a list of questions, or survey instrument. The surveyor records information on the basis of the on-site interview. You may want to use direct intercept research to gather opinions from students, alumni, parents, townspeople, or faculty.

Since the interviews are person-to-person, this method has special advantages in gathering responses to prototypes—for example, viewbook cover designs. Of course, as the degree of personal contact increases, the cost of the survey method increases. Thus, intercept research requires more time and labor than telephone or mail research. But, if the survey is structured properly, the responses will offer proportionately more depth.

• *Personal interviews* help in obtaining in-depth, detailed information. These one-on-one interviews allow the surveyor to pursue questions in great detail with specific individuals. Since this method allows you to choose your own respondents, you would want to use it in cases where a specific person's in-depth opinions are particularly valuable. For example, you might use personal interviews to gather information from your president, deans, or key trustees.

Personal interview is, of course, the most time- and labor-intensive survey method of those listed here, and thus the most expensive. Still, used correctly, it should provide proportionately more valuable information.

Whatever methods you choose, sound marketing research requires that you:

1. Identify the problem. Why are you embarking on this research project?

2. Develop the research instrument. What questions will you ask? In what form?

3. Test the research project on a representative random sample from your target audience. Evaluate the test results, and modify the instrument as necessary.

4. Perform the survey, monitoring the process carefully.

5. Evaluate the results and analyze the data.

6. Report the findings.

7. Apply the findings to your image-building campaign.

One of the most useful studies your institution could conduct would be to poll a number of audiences (on campus and off) using a semantic differential scale. Audiences would rank the institution on such scales as friendly/unfriendly, innovative/stodgy, warm/cool, rigorous/easy, and so on. Here again, your institution can also study how your audiences view competitors. The information you gather will help define your institution's market position.

If you decide that some kinds of research are beyond the skills and abilities of your in-house staff, you may want to consider an outside firm. Many such service firms advertise in journals of higher education and have display booths at educational meetings and conventions. Be sure to talk with some of the previous clients of the firms before making a decision.

Don't ignore independent studies that may apply to your institution. For example, in 1982, 1983, and 1984, Group Attitudes Corporation, a division of Hill and Knowlton, Inc., designed and conducted national surveys of public attitudes toward higher education. The 1982 survey discovered that fewer than two in 10 Americans (17 percent) rated mass media (newspapers, magazines, television, and radio) as very important sources of information about higher education. Personal contacts, counselors, faculty members, publications, commercial guidebooks, and orientation programs were deemed more important sources of information. (This is why communications are so important to your image program.) College publications in particular received high recognition as valuable information sources. *American Attitudes Toward Higher Education,* the survey results, are available (see bibliography). The reports are excellent samples of market survey methodology and a source of ideas for applying these research techniques to your institution.

Step II: Understand your institution

As an institutional advancement professional, you are responsible for ensuring that image creation is ethical, honest, truthful, and in the best interests of your target audiences. CASE has published a Statement of Ethics for institutional advancement, which is an excellent model and guide for individuals and institutions planning image creation campaigns.

Whatever the nature of your institution, you must market reality. The danger of doing otherwise does exist, and you must be sensitive to it. *Don't be tempted to create false images not based in solid fact.* An institution that engages in false image creation will pay the price in the long run.

You cannot establish and successfully maintain a positive image for an institution that does not, in fact, deserve that image. Image depends upon the quality of the institution itself. You cannot impose a new image on old Siwash U (poor programs, poor location, poor administration, poor faculty, poor students, poor esprit) and hope to compete in the Ivy League. If you try, the opposite may happen. An old adage runs: "The best way to kill a bad program is to market it." False image projection may in fact accelerate failure.

The key, then, is to truly understand your institution, its aims and objectives. Imagine that you are working with *products.* Each course, major, curriculum, department, school, college, and university may be thought of as a product. You can market these individually or collectively. Each has its strengths and weaknesses. Understand your products, audience needs, and the competitive marketplace before you try to influence how your institution is perceived.

Statement of Ethics

Institutional advancement professionals, by virtue of their special responsibilities within the academic community, represent their colleges, universities, and schools to the larger society. They have, therefore, a special duty to exemplify the best qualities of their institutions, and to observe the highest standards of personal and professional conduct.

In so doing, they promote the merits of their institutions, and of education generally, without disparaging other colleges and schools;

Their words and actions embody respect for truth, fairness, free inquiry, and the opinions of others;

They respect all individuals without regard to race, color, sex, creed, ethnic or national identity, handicap, or age;

They uphold the professional reputation of other advancement officers, and give credit for ideas, words, or images originated by others;

They safeguard privacy rights and confidential information;

They do not grant or accept favors for personal gain, nor do they solicit or accept favors for their institutions where a higher public interest would be violated;

They avoid actual or apparent conflicts of interest, and, if in doubt, seek guidance from appropriate authorities;

They follow the letter and spirit of laws and regulations affecting institutional advancement;

They observe these standards and others that apply to their professions, and actively encourage colleagues to join them in supporting the highest standards of conduct.

The CASE Board of Trustees adopted this Statement of Ethics to guide and reinforce our professional conduct in all areas of institutional advancement. The statement is also intended to stimulate awareness and discussion of ethical issues that may arise in our professional activities. The Board adopted the final text in Toronto on July 11, 1982, after a year's deliberation by national and district leaders and by countless volunteers throughout the membership.

Step III: Establish comparative differential advantage

Imagine a cold glass of lemonade and a hot cup of coffee. They are similar (both are beverages). They are also different (one is made from lemons, the other from coffee beans; one is hot, the other cold). But when it comes to marketing, the most important thing is not the lemonade or the coffee itself. It's the user's *needs*. A hot cup of coffee may be just the thing on a cold winter morning. A cold glass of lemonade hits the spot when you've come in from weeding the garden.

This example illustrates *comparative differential advantage*. It's your responsibility to identify comparative differential advantages for your institution and its components and to build images around them. With this idea, you can begin to differentiate your products from others that, on first glance, seem similar in the eyes of your target audience. Apply public relations, marketing, and communications skills to promoting these differences, and you're on the road to success.

For example, your institution may be an independent school. Market research (and enrollment statistics) may indicate that you have strengths in the fine arts; perhaps theater and dance are dominant. You would create an image mix highlighting those areas. That focus is your institution's comparative differential advantage over competing institutions.

By comparison, your institution may be a large university. Your institution may have theater and dance courses as part of its College of Liberal Arts, but market research shows that the university's strengths are in the College of Engineering. More specifically, perhaps the strongest programs in your College of Engineering are mechanical engineering and computer sciences. These products, then, are your institution's comparative differential advantage, and they should form a focus for your institutional image.

Then, by building on your institution's strengths, you will be able to find ways to introduce some of your institution's other components. You can actually improve the images of your secondary programs by letting them "ride on the coattails" of stronger ones.

Here's one technique you may use to define a comparative differential advantage:

Start with small components within your institution. For a community college, these could be individual courses. For a large, complex university, these could be core curricula or majors. Work with faculty and staff to determine current strengths. Focus attention on curricular and service development: What new courses, services, or programs are planned? Can you identify new directions? Make note of key words used to describe these components. List them.

Do the same thing at the next level. If you began with services or courses, now work with departments. Interview department heads. List the key words they use to describe their departments.

At the college level, ask the dean of the college to describe his or her institution. List key words.

Now, put the words together. Create short phrases, sentences, and paragraphs. You will begin to form an editorial picture of your institution. Examine this picture critically. Are ideas specific? Can they be used to position your institution and its components in the marketplace? Will the picture help your image for admissions? development? alumni work? community relations? continuing education? sponsored research? mass media?

As an example, let's create a word-description model for a mythical school, the Valley School of the Performing Arts.

> The Valley School of the Performing Arts is an academic component of Southern Lutheran University located in Phoenix, Arizona. Its goals, as Dean Morris Terwilliger describes them, are "to offer programs in the performing arts, particularly theater and dance" and "to become the strongest undergraduate arts program in the Southwestern United States." Southern Lutheran University supports the programs with income from the Marvin P. Banknote Endowment for the Arts. The late Mr. Banknote's legacy is dedicated to sustaining a strong undergraduate academic program in performing arts.

> As part of a larger institution, Southern Lutheran University, the Valley School of the Performing Arts is able to enroll 1,150 students in a four-year undergraduate program. Financial aid is available for many students.

> The dance program focuses, in particular, on musical performance and ballet. Highlights of the program include an opportunity for six months of study with a professional European dance tour group. The program also includes a special Freshman Performing Group. This dance company performs at the Phoenix Dance Theater and appears in the Phoenix Dance Festival each spring. It is the school's way of contributing to the cultural life of the local community.

> Graduates are members of such prestigious dance groups as the American Ballet Theater, the Joffrey Ballet, and the New York City Ballet. Alumni have formed Alumni Performing Arts Groups in New York City, Miami, Denver, San Francisco, and Dallas/Fort Worth. They have been active in recruiting new students and in fund raising.

> Academic focus for the future is on the incorporation of "synthetic music" (computer-generated sounds) to dance and performance. A chair has been established to sponsor an annual faculty position to compose for this study, an integral part of the school's dance program. This gives the program a distinct advantage over that of ABC University, the institution's primary competitor.

> The Valley School is located in the desert near Scottsdale. Besides enjoying the obvious advantage of natural beauty and the surrounding Superstition Mountains, the school's buildings are designed as stage settings for outdoor dance performances. Often choreographed for nighttime presentation, these events are spectacles of beauty—dramatic lighting reveals natural scenery juxtaposed with human forms in motion.

Just as you can create word pictures of an institution's components, you can prepare a composite word picture of the parent institution. These descriptions can be used to weave image ideas into such editorial projects as news releases, president's speeches, viewbooks, slide shows, advertisements, and so on.

Once the words and ideas begin to reveal a comparative differential advantage for your institution, you need to translate these ideas into visuals.

What photographic opportunities do the words suggest? How can you capture them for television? slide shows? illustrations? Develop a library of black-and-white and color photographs that support the editorial concepts you have collected. You can use words and visuals together to communicate the institution's image and comparative differential advantage. You might also create a library of audio sounds (actualities) that reflect the editorial pictures.

As you begin creating an image with this approach, you are starting global institutional marketing, as described in the last chapter. Since some apects of your institution's components are common, your efforts in one area (for example, admissions) begin to assist efforts in another area (for example, development).

Step IV: Involve people in an image/marketing plan

Conduct an audit of your outreach materials as described in Chapter 1. Analyze the needs of your constituents. Use research to gather information on your institution's image. Then prepare a presentation of your findings for your institution's leadership. Use the materials you have gathered to illustrate the need for a coordinated image program.

Consider asking the president or vice president to create a task force to work on image improvement. If you go this route, select committee members carefully to represent institutional interest groups and different points of view. The task force should be a working group, not a rubber-stamp committee. Consider involving faculty, administrators, staff, students, and outside representatives (trustees, alumni, etc.).

It's important to communicate. Make sure internal administrators and staff understand the importance of institutional image. Determine their needs. How do those needs relate to your image objectives and institutional marketing plan? Describe how image improvement will help them. Make clear how combining and targeting all efforts will both increase their impact and save money.

Your greatest resource is the people who will work with you to measure, evaluate, plan, and execute your institutional image project.

Of course, there is no set plan for executing an image program. You must create your own plan based on your institution's situation, opportunities, and limitations. We'll discuss this in more detail in Chapter 7.

Step V: Measure, evaluate, maintain—and refine as necessary

Once you have launched a comprehensive image plan with global institutional attributes, you will begin to reap the fruits of your labors. It's easy, at that point, to let the whole project drop. You must not let that happen. Image building is a combination of short-term successes that result in long-term improvement.

Consider ways to use research to measure image improvement. Evaluate progress. Find every possible way to propagate and maintain the positive image you (and others) have created.

Still, despite your hard work and best efforts to create a new positive institutional image, you should not be surprised if your program needs some refinements. Be prepared to make adjustments as your image program develops. Remember that your institution will change. That's inevitable. The image you create should change in concert with the institution.

The image development process at work

Suppose research indicates that an audience—say, parents and potential students—has a negative image of your institution, perhaps as a result of past problems.

How can you use these steps for image creation to replace ideas that are negative or out-of-date?

As stated in the introduction, an institution's image depends upon *the quality, scope, and effectiveness of its academic programs.* In order to change an institution's image, actions must precede or accompany words.

Richard W. Moll, formerly dean of admissions at the University of California at Santa Cruz, describes a real-life example.

Santa Cruz, he says, was "the institutional flower child" of the '60s and '70s, "nurtured as a '60s reaction to the multicampus UC system." Founded in 1965, the institution was an extension of the times, with "narratives instead of grades, do-it-yourself majors, and the like." The experiment flourished until a wave of conservatism swept the country. Parents and students became preoccupied with vocational and practical education, and enrollments plummeted.

To combat the problem, Santa Cruz began with market research. "Students, parents, and counselors throughout California filled out questionnaires to guide Santa Cruz in altering a gone-wrong image," Moll writes. "The findings were consistent: Although famous for [its] beautiful location, UCSC had also become well-known for 'no grades,' questionable academic rigor, and a laid-back, Californian, 'sensitivity' approach."

Dean Moll tells how an off-campus retreat helped officials "decide on the essence of the 'new' Santa Cruz message. The message had to be true to the place, of course, but it also had to emphasize the rigor, the quite successful graduate school placement, and the actual role of 'experimentation.' " He described reducing the college story to six key words: undergraduate, hybrid, atmosphere, traditional, rigorous, and selective.

Moll developed an image plan that included renovating a building on campus for admissions visitors, buying a bus for use in campus tours, training recruiters to present the new image at high schools, organizing alumni and parents to help with recruitment, hosting conferences on campus for counselors, and giving personal lectures about the college. Besides creating a new editorial approach based on the six key words, Moll was instrumental in revamping many targeted publications to communicate new words and visuals, centered around the slogan "An Ideal Becoming Real." The rest is history: Santa Cruz has emerged as an educational leader with a new image.

You can follow Santa Cruz's example of applying image-building principles to replace old ideas. *New, consistent, and accurate information can replace old conceptions or misconceptions.* This can be difficult, however, and requires dedicated efforts over a long period of time. And once you have established the image you and other institutional leaders seek, don't relax. You must maintain the image, because images (like the institution and its components) are always changing, evolving, and being reassessed in the receiver's mind.

To summarize:

1. How can you use research to assess, improve, create, and maintain a positive institutional image? component images?

2. How can you better understand your institution in order to plan and create an image campaign?

3. How can you determine your institution's comparative differential advantage? How can you identify and communicate comparative differential advantage to target audiences?

4. How can you involve the appropriate people in developing an institutional image program? How do you institute and execute your image plan?

5. How can you measure, evaluate, and maintain your image program? What is necessary to refine your image after you have researched and created it?

---

[1] See "Kent State University: Coping with an Image Crisis," by Bruce H. Allen, associate professor of marketing, De Paul University, in *Cases and Readings for Marketing for Nonprofit Organizations,* pp. 249-263.

[2] Richard W. Moll, "A Flower Child Grows Up: Responding to changing times at UC Santa Cruz," CURRENTS (November/December 1983), pp. 16-18.

Part III

Marketing and Institutional Image

Chapter 7

The Four R's of Image-making

More than a decade ago, Philip Kotler, who holds the Harold T. Martin Professorship at Northwestern University, first described how marketing principles could be applied to nonprofit organizations.

In his book, *Marketing for Nonprofit Organizations,* Kotler suggested that non-profit organizations apply approaches that had traditionally been used to market "hard" or "tangible" products. He described the "four P" approach: Product, Price, Promotion, and Place. His ideas revolutionized the ways nonprofit organizations thought about themselves, and his concepts have been adopted by nonprofit groups ranging from colleges and universities to health-care organizations, city governments, religious organizations, political parties, museums, symphony orchestras, libraries, and zoos.

You must understand and apply marketing's four P's before you attempt to embark on image research, creation, control, maintenance, and propagation.

With homage to Kotler, I have created a set of ideas for institutional image advancement similar to the four-P concept. I call these the "four R's." They are Research, Recognition, Repetition, and Recollection.

Research

Nonprofit organizations have classically maintained a product-based orientation rather than a marketing orientation, which is consumer-related and service-based. That is, they determine what they are good at doing and encourage people to use those services or products. The approach has been passive, not active.

It is important to consider what services you are best at providing (Kotler's Product). But that alone is not sufficient. You must augment this "inside-out" approach with an "outside-in" approach. Institutions must start with the audience. They must first assess consumer needs, identify demands, and then generate or adapt products targeted to meet those demands.

Research is the way to determine current and future consumer demands and needs. You can use qualitative and quantitative research to measure consumer attitudes, image perceptions, and success of your institution's products (services). Research that combines market information about customers and competitors with survey information about what people want and are willing to pay for (or, in the case of development, are willing to donate to) can provide a firm base for planning for change.

Market research can be complex and difficult. Start by assessing in-house capabilities. Your organization may have staff members with experience in market research, computer analysis, or research interpretation and strategy development. If the necessary background and skills are not available, hiring outside commercial market research firms may be the best way to proceed. It's often more effective to examine an institution from the outside than from within.

Market research is often expensive. Be sure to get comprehensive estimates for the work you need. Outline any aspects to be done in-house. The final proposal should describe what is to be done, who is to do it, and the price.

When you start discussing research in higher education, you raise a sensitive issue: How much should colleges and universities respond to market forces? The corporate sector uses research to measure a product's life cycle. A corporate product goes through development, acceptance, maturity, and decline. When the product reaches the area of decline, it is dropped or a new product is created to take its place.

In higher education, the issue is not so clear-cut. Should an institution be market-driven and provide products to match consumer demands? Or should the institution stick to its tried-and-true curriculum, thus, in effect, deciding what is best for the consumer? Should an institution phase out courses and programs in, say, Latin and logic, in favor of computer science? How should faculty respond? administrators? students? parents? alumni?

These issues vary from institution to institution. A community college might create and drop courses as the market dictates. But an Ivy League university may have a different attitude about phasing out its classics department!

There are no easy answers to these questions. These issues provide one more reason to make sure that you and others involved in marketing and image decisions understand both your institution in particular and higher education's missions and traditions in general.

When the market research is completed and you have a report on the findings, you are ready for the next step. Share the report with your president or chancellor, board, key administrators, and staff members. You may want to make a special presentation to your student body leaders. Describe the plans for implementation. Follow through. Too often, carefully conducted market research ends up in a report that is put on the shelf and forgotten. To be useful, market research should be implemented immediately. The findings are perishable, and will need to be updated.

The ABC Paradox: A Case for Research

Administrators working at ABC University had, over the years, become painfully aware of the problems the university experienced as a result of its urban location. ABC is located in the middle of one of America's largest cities. Safety problems for students and staff, a high crime rate, a deteriorating physical plant, and housing and transportation problems seemed significant. Administrators agreed that higher education and urban deterioration were not compatible.

Administrators made conscious and unconscious decisions to overlook the fact that ABC was located in the midst of a thriving, active metropolis. Printed materials hardly mentioned the city and its various qualities and attractions.

Declining applications for admission forced top administrators to invite an outside consultant to campus. The consultant and his firm, which specialized in marketing research and communications for higher education, conducted a study. It focused on measuring the attitudes of student applicants, matriculants, and nonmatriculants (those who had, despite expressing original interest in ABC University, decided to go elsewhere). The administrators eagerly awaited the research results and resulting marketing plan.

Research often produces unexpected results. In this case, it revealed that one of ABC's best features, according to current students, was its *location*! Most students responded positively to the fact that the institution was in a busy city. They enjoyed the resources a large city provided—its museums, theatres, libraries, professional organizations, and reputation. They also saw the city as the hub of international activities. It was, in fact, one of the main reasons they had chosen ABC!

The consultant urged the university to focus on its urban location in its promotional outreach materials. The president and other top administrators approved a change in direction. New photography captured the urban environment and its advantages. The campus map, changed to include all of the city, identified major cultural, academic, and entertainment resources. What had been considered a liability turned into a major asset.

The ABC paradox is a lesson for many institutions. It reminds us that:

1. Agreement (by internal staff) may compound a problem rather than provide a solution.

2. One must look at an institution from the outside, not just from the inside.

3. Research is the best tool to help define an institution's image.

Recognition

We like to be recognized by friends when we're in a crowd. For an educational institution, too, recognition is critical. The marketplace is a crowded arena buzzing with competition, where many institutions vie for attention and recognition.

In Chapter 1, I described two theories about image. One suggested that image was product-determined; that is, that it depended on attributes of the institution. The other suggested that image was person-determined—a result of audience perceptions. I concluded that image was most likely formed as a combination of both internal and external factors.

Recognition is a result of the "marriage" of these two ideas. It occurs in the perceiver's mind when the product-determined image matches or supports the person-determined image. When this happens the product—your institution—stands out. The institution gains advantage over competitors in the competitive marketplace.

Corporate marketers refer to audience recognition and perception of their products as "product differentiation." Each product is packaged and marketed with an eye to product differentiation—recognition of the product, perceptions of the product's attributes, and the image of the product in relation to the competition.

How do consumers recognize products? What sets one apart while others are lost in the competitive arena? What factors lead to institutional recognition? How can we help our institutions gain this? How can communications and media contribute to institutional recognition? What affords one institution primary consumer recognition while another institution appears secondary?

Each institution, each situation, will have a different set of answers to these questions. The important thing is to make sure that you keep asking the questions—frequently. Answers will come from a marketing strategy; strategy grows out of market research. Your job is to make sure the questions are asked and that answers are carefully interpreted, evaluated, re-evaluated, and applied.

Recognition is the glue that binds your institution and its programs and activities to a target audience member's mind. It requires the development of a carefully orchestrated image based on your institution's strengths. The best way to improve recognition is to present a clear, unified total image. Consumers will find it easier to focus on and recognize an institution if they can associate a clear image with the institution's name.

Remember this especially when you promote component parts of an institution. Constituents become confused when components are identified individually at the expense of the parent organization. For example, ABC University may have an aggressive department of fine arts, called the Dali School of Fine Arts. If the Dali School of Fine Arts always identified itself (say, on its letterhead or in a schedule of courses) without identifying ABC University, the consumer would become more aware of the component (Dali School of Fine Arts) than of the parent organization (ABC University). That is, the consumer might recognize the Dali School, but that recognition, no matter how positive, would not improve recognition for the university.

I call this *marketing self-destruction* through self-imposed fragmentation. Educational institutions have a dismal record of doing this, either intentionally or unintentionally. The simple idea of *collective* rather than individual component identity is critical to the long-term effects of image building and image recognition.

Repetition

One of the best ways to learn something is to repeat it. Grade school teachers know that repetition helps the student remember. Corporate advertisers know that it is important to repeat the product's name. Many television commercials repeat the product's name over and over. (Most of us are painfully aware of this repetition!) That is not done by accident. There are, for radio commercials and other media, "rules" about how many times the product name must be repeated in order to plant the product in the consumer's mind. Even print ads show product name repetition.

Pay careful attention to commercial product promotion. Study the ways product names are repeated to gain consumer recognition.

A note of caution: Educational institutions should be careful *not* to adopt offensive or questionable commercial techniques. Promotion should be done in good taste with a sensitivity for the ideals that are important to education, the institution, and its audiences.

Let's examine ways that you can use repetition to achieve a positive institutional image. To begin with, repetition can help you maintain consistency in the ideas and images you communicate. You can use a well-designed logo or symbol repeatedly to communicate a consistent idea. Similarly, editorial concepts or key words (see Chapter 6) can be repeated in various vehicles (news releases, viewbooks, advertisements, and speeches, for example).

Explore opportunities to repeat identifying concepts about your institution. What opportunities exist? Can ideas, concepts, and visuals be piggy-backed on existing outreach materials? What new materials can you create to repeat key ideas? Seek every opportunity to deliver concise and consistent images.

For example, consider the situation of many state university systems. One obvious marketing and image building advantage for a state college or university is its relationship to a parent organization or system. Since component institutions within a system often share in part the same name, the concept of repetition plays a particularly important role here—both for the individual institutions and the system as a whole.

Take the New York State university system, for instance: State University of New York at Albany, State University of New York at Binghamton, and so on. Thanks to this name relationship, each institution's visibility magnifies when any other "sister" institution is mentioned. That is, when one component repeats the system's name, both the system as a whole and every component in the system benefit from the repetition.

Of course, as with all image-building techniques, this sort of repetition will help only if the system is perceived as being of high quality. An institution that is part of a system perceived as poor in quality will carry the burden of that perception—

and repetition of the system's name in the institution's name will increase that burden. On the other hand, if the institution itself can develop a positive image, it may be able to improve the system image as a whole. Thus, one very strong university, might, by association, support the images of several other institutions that share a system name.

Recollection

When you hear the words "expensive imported automobile," what brand do you think of? When you hear "domestic airline service," what airline do you think of? What brand of television set? What overnight letter and package delivery service? What Ivy League institution? What state university? What women's college? What independent school? What hospital? What zoo?

Why do you recall one product, institution, or service over another? How do you classify these in your memory? When do you reclassify one above another?

Corporate marketers, advertising personnel, and public relations staff have studied these questions for decades. As usual, there are no easy answers; these questions go to the core of our mental processes.

We do know that the idea of recollection is important to marketing. Millions of dollars are spent every week to try to keep one product ahead of the other in the consumer's mind.

Think back to what we learned about associative memory in Chapter 3. Every person will associate particular concepts with particular institutions; when you hear such terms as "Ivy League" or "fine arts institute," your memory will produce the name of an individual institution that, for some personal reason, stands out above the rest. Similarly, when you hear the name of an institution, your mind may see it as representative of a whole class of similar institutions. In building an image for an institution, your goal is to encourage audience members to think of your institution as representing a particular positive type.

There is great power in the idea of recollection. The degree to which your audiences recall your institution and its programs and activities, as well as how accurately these images relate to reality, and how they compare with competitors, are measures of the effectiveness of your institution's image-building program.

How can your institution achieve recollection in the minds of your target audiences? Probably the best way is to continually strive to deliver the best product in response to your target audience's needs. That's a simple idea, but one that's difficult to achieve. But it lies at the core of any image-building program. As I've mentioned before, you can't build an image without basing it on substance.

Of the 3,000 or so institutions of higher education in the United States, only a handful will come to the mind of any member of your target audience. Look at those institutions as models; seek out the ones closest in type to your own. What can you learn from them?

In summary, let's review some key ideas to help your institution apply the four R's of image making.

1. How can you develop and apply *research* to build your institution's image? How can an "outside-in" approach help your institution learn about itself?

2. How can your institution achieve *recognition* in the competitive marketplace? What practical ideas can you apply to help improve recognition?

3. How can you use *repetition* in your image-building program? Consider possibilities for your parent organization as well as components.

4. *Recollection* suggests a focus in the minds of target audience members. What can you do, through image building, to improve your institution's degree of recognition to encourage recollection?

Chapter 8

Positioning Your Institution

An institution's position, as I described earlier, is its stature in relation to competing institutions, as perceived by its target audiences. We use the term *institutional positioning* to describe our efforts to control our institutions' placement in the marketplace. That term, however, is imprecise. In positioning, we do not change our institutions; rather, we attempt to alter the perceptions in the minds of our audience members. Technically, we might refer to this process as "constituent cerebral positioning."

We exist in a competitive society. You must remember that your products (courses, curricula, majors, programs, entertainment, activities, schools, colleges, and universities) exist in a competitive marketplace. The marketplace is the arena of people's minds—the minds of current constituents and target audiences. Their perception of your institution is critical. The collective perceptions—your institution's image—determine your institution's position. Keep in mind that you can position anything, be it a course, a curriculum, a major, an activity, a capital campaign, a school, an individual, a college, a university, or a state educational network.

Every institution strives to be best, but of course no institution can be best in everything. Institutions may, however, have strengths in certain services, curricula, programs, or activities.

Let's look at the corporate sector. Some years ago, many corporations boasted that their products were "best" or "first." In today's corporate marketing world, however, corporations use comparatives, not superlatives, to describe their products' advantages.

For instance, Avis is No. 2 in rental cars. Honeywell is the "other computer company." Seven-Up® is the "Uncola." Each description positions the corporate product relative to competing products.

It can be unwise for institutions of higher education to market themselves in similar ways: "XYZ College's educational programs are almost as good as Harvard's." But you can use positioning strategy to emphasize connections that already exist in the viewer's mind, or to build new conections—based, of course, on quality and reality.

For example, Carnegie-Mellon University in Pittsburgh has always been perceived as an excellent institution for engineering studies. To strengthen its position in the educational marketplace, Carnegie-Mellon several years ago launched a program to equip all of its students with computers and to promote computer literacy in many fields of study. These efforts have gained the institution prominence in the fields of computer application and education. But, equally important, these efforts have been the focus for a new image. By capitalizing on the computer study ideas, Carnegie-Mellon improved its position in the marketplace. It is now seen as an institution with a strong focus on computer application in many areas of study, not just those associated with engineering.

Competing with communications

Less is more. In Germany, in the 1920s, the Bauhaus design school promoted this theory. We can apply the idea as well to institutional positioning through image development.

We live in an overcommunicated society. Thousands of competitive editorial, visual, and aural messages bombard us daily. Research proves that your mind defends itself against the volume of communication thrust at it. It screens, rejects, accepts, and classifies information. In general, your mind accepts only that which agrees with your prior knowledge or experience.

Receivers have trouble taking in complicated messages and information. So your aim should be to communicate in simple, easy-to-understand terms. Your institution must find ways to distill complex philosophical concepts into ideas that you can communicate simply and easily. The process should focus on the receiver's mind. How will audience members perceive your messages?

Take the Carnegie-Mellon example. The idea of computers is an excellent adjunct for academic programs normally not associated with computer application. It can be communicated simply and positively. And, since it was novel at that time, the news media helped spread the word.

Many forms of media provide vehicles for your institutional image messages: television (commercial, cable, and pay), radio (AM and FM), posters, publications, billboards, newspapers (daily, weekly, and Sunday), local shopping guides, magazines (consumer magazines, alumni magazines, and so on), and even cards or posters in and on buses, trucks, streetcars, subways, and taxis. Even the human body can become a media vehicle for your institution. Just think of the messages carried by T-shirts and monograms.

Still, your messages will encounter severe competition for visibility in the marketplace. A *media mix*—the selection of appropriate forms of media to reach specific target audiences—is critical to establish your institution's position.

Timing is important. Saying the right things to the right people at the right time and place helps to build your image and position your institution. Carnegie-Mellon's early adoption of computers for each student positioned it as an innovator. Those universities that acted two or three years later gained little or nothing in image.

What should you promote?

Imagine a scale that describes your institutional image by levels:

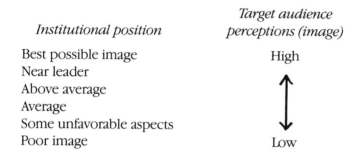

Institutional position	Target audience perceptions (image)
Best possible image	High
Near leader	
Above average	
Average	
Some unfavorable aspects	
Poor image	Low

Table 1. Image Levels

Market research may determine that your institution is low on the scale. Assuming your product justifies the effort, your job is to move the target audience's perceptions up the scale. This movement is called image enhancement.

Image enhancement prototypes exist in the corporate world. Consider Volkswagen.® For years Detroit auto manufacturers were producing and promoting big cars. Volkswagen marketed a small, ugly car. Possible marketing strategies might have been to position the VW Beetle as a "big" car by using wide-angle photography, or to promote reliability or gas mileage. VW chose to focus on the honest fact. Its most successful ad had a simple, straight-forward photo of the product and a two-word headline: "Think small."

David Ogilvy, a successful advertising consultant for corporations, once said, "Every advertisement is a long-term investment in the image of a product." He proved his statement with campaigns for Hathaway shirts, Rolls-Royce, Schweppes, and other products.

Conceivably, a large institution might choose an image and positioning approach that focuses on institutional diversity. That is, promotion would center on the fact that the institution offers more choice than its competitors do. However, this is a difficult idea to communicate effectively. Corporations have found it hard to build a position based on diversity; approaches emphasizing specific strengths have been much more successful.

Many corporations select an image-building concept that presents an overall parent image in conjunction with specific service, product, or component images. Consider, for example, Beatrice Corporation, one of the world's leading diversified food companies. Beatrice deals in dairy beverages, groceries, food distribution

tribution and warehousing, speciality meats, confections and snacks, agricultural products, and chemical and allied products. Under this corporate umbrella of services, the corporation offers products with brand names such as Tropicana, Swiss Miss, La Choy, Fisher, Eckrich, Samsonite, Arrowhead, Great Bear, Ozarka, Rosarita, Aunt Nellie's, Martha White, Butterkrust, Culligan, LouverDrape, Day-Timers, Converters Ink (printing inks), Craig Adhesives, Farboil (marine coatings), Stahl (leather finishes), and LNP (engineering plastics), among others. Each of these products has its own image within its own market; all, however, are identified on a larger scale with Beatrice Corporation.

Here are some ideas an institution might use—alone or in combination—to establish a position in the marketplace.

1. *Product strengths.* What courses, majors, services, or curricula are truly outstanding and consistently attract consumers? Where are your institution's strongest points? Why? Product strengths may include some of the noncurricular aspects of your institution (location, campus beauty, tradition, campus life, and so on).

2. *Research leadership.* What special areas of research have enjoyed recognition? Why? What potential areas exist? Why?

3. *Service leadership.* Does your institution excel in serving your city, state, or region? Perhaps your outstanding agricultural extension service sets you apart, or your internationally known medical center.

4. *Placement leadership.* What are successful alumni doing? What are the placement statistics for the last graduating class? What have graduates gone on to do?

5. *Satisfied customers.* What are former constituents saying about your institution? Why?

These are simple ideas. But a position, built on careful research, image planning, development, and maintenance, could be established from this plan. Many other ideas and combinations of ideas are possible. Your planning should combine broad objectives (global institutional marketing) as well as specific objectives (image development for a single service, course, or curriculum). The latter should support the former.

To summarize:

1. What position does your institution have in the competitive marketplace? What positions do competitors have?

2. How can you use image development to improve your position?

3. What methods of communication (media mix) will achieve the most visibility for your institution?

4. What specific areas (services, courses, curricula, development, sports activities, community relations, grants development, staff skills) could you use to establish a position in the marketplace?

Chapter 9

Implementing a Marketing Plan

C an an institution create or change its image without using marketing techniques? This concept of image development as marketing may produce some confusion in the educational world. But image development and marketing go hand-in-hand—in fact, a coordinated, total marketing plan is essential to building a cohesive image.

Many institutions are developing marketing plans to solve problems, to head off possible problems, or simply to improve their positions in the competitive nonprofit marketplace. Marketing is not a panacea. But, for many educational institutions, it can spell the difference between success and failure.

What should you do when your institution needs a marketing plan? Who should initiate the plan? Who should be involved? What results can you expect, and how can you measure them? How will your plan relate to your institution's image? Where do you begin?

There is no *one* place where a marketing plan begins. It could start in any office—admissions, development, public relations, community affairs—and at any level of administration. The important thing is that it begins someplace.

One of the best ways to get a marketing program started is to perform an image audit of your institution's outreach publications, as described in Chapter 1. Gather materials intended for your institution's audiences: recruitment brochures, direct mail solicitations, staff and alumni periodicals, the mission statement, advertisements, and so on. Spread these materials out on a large table, and take a long hard look at them.

If your institution has a coordinated image program, these materials will look like they belong together. Each piece will include vital information about the institution. Each will have clear visual, graphic, and editorial continuity. Each will target information to discrete audiences. And each will help position your institution in the competitive educational marketplace.

Of course, image development depends upon much more than coordinated outreach materials. Remember, the executive leadership of your institution plays an important role in its image. So does the quality and character of its curricula, its faculty, and its students. So do media relations, community relations programs, and internal communications.

An institution may lack coordinated publications and still create a highly positive image. For example, an institution strong in scientific or technical fields might rely on effective media relations, using stories in major newspapers and appearances on radio and TV to show the institution as a leader in its fields. An Ivy League university might have a completely uncoordinated graphic image, but enjoy an outstanding overall image on the basis of the long-term excellence of its programs.

Still, if your institution does not have a total strategy in place, the materials on the table will make that obvious. The publications will appear uncoordinated, unrelated, or even conflicting. This is a strong sign that your institution needs a comprehensive marketing and image-building plan.

How to activate your campus

You may be able to use the materials you have collected to illustrate your institution's need for a coordinated marketing and image-building plan.

Start by enlisting the support of people you work with—the president, appropriate vice presidents, faculty, board members. Once you've piqued their interest, look into holding a meeting of the most influential people on campus. Create a presentation to explain the reasons for developing a marketing plan. (You might convert some of the publications you've collected into color slides to show them.)

You may want to tell these people that a consistent marketing approach—global institutional marketing—brings results greater than the simple total of the parts. Consider including concepts from Philip Kotler's book, *Marketing for Nonprofit Organizations,* which explains how marketing concepts and strategies apply to the nonprofit field. You may want to summarize his ideas about audience segmentation, positioning, competition, research, or the four P's (product, price, place, and promotion). You may want to include ideas from my book *Marketing Higher Education: A Practical Guide.*

Above all, it's important to describe the results you can expect from a well-developed marketing plan. The plan should bring direct benefit to everyone in your audience. You should make clear what those benefits are, and how combining and targeting your efforts will increase their impact and, perhaps, save money.

Who to involve

A well-executed marketing plan will touch the lives and activities of practically everyone at your institution at one time or another. It's important, then, to involve as many people as possible.

Involve the opinion leaders. Who are the key board members? faculty? administrators? students? alumni? Do any faculty members in your business school have an interest in marketing educational institutions? A word of caution: the concepts of marketing nonprofit organizations are quite new—barely a dozen years old—so don't be surprised if some of your suggestions meet with blank stares!

Different campuses choose different approaches. Some form marketing committees. Others rely on a central individual to introduce marketing concepts. You may want to create a task force to study marketing opportunities on your campus. The best method for your institution will reflect its academic, political, administrative, and managerial environment.

Creating the marketing plan

As Figure 5 shows, marketing and image building is a cyclical process that begins and ends with research. From the beginning, market research helps you assess the needs, perceptions, and attitudes of your target audiences. It can be invaluable in

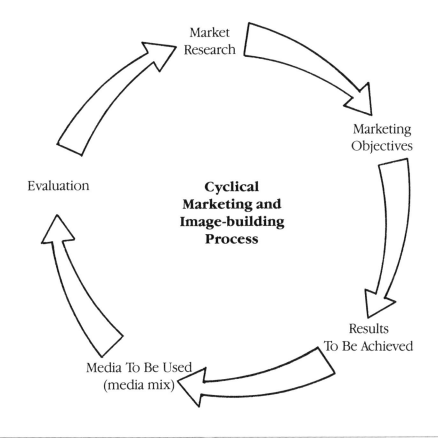

Figure 5: The Marketing and Image-building Cycle

providing the framework for planning marketing, for implementing a marketing and image plan, and for evaluating a plan after it's implemented. And follow-up research can suggest changes in marketing approaches to make them more efficient and effective.

The best marketing plans describe both objectives and methods for all appropriate areas within the institution. Your plan may include strategies for the academic area, admissions, alumni, development, student affairs, community relations, public relations, government relations—or any other areas important to your institutional image.

The marketing plan for each of these institutional components should follow the same basic outline:

1. *Research.* Describe conclusions gathered from market research as they relate to the component as well as to the parent institution. Note relationships and implications of the research.

2. *Planning assumptions.* State directly the institution's missions and the plans for the component to clarify the component's direction for the future.

3. *Goals.* Describe the institution's goals for the component.

4. *Objectives.* List the component's ambitions, in order of priority. Compare institutional goals with component ambitions. Are they compatible? If not, consider ways to resolve differences.

5. *Target audiences.* Identify the component's target audiences. The list may include primary, secondary, and tertiary audience groups. Compare your lists to determine overlap.

6. *Strategies.* Discuss the logical approaches for reaching target audiences in order to achieve your marketing goals and objectives. Derive your strategies from studying the first five items on this list.

7. *Media mix.* Suggest a combination of "vehicles" for delivering your marketing strategies. These media may differ from component to component in order to take advantage of the most efficient and effective means of communication.

Bear in mind that the individual and collective strategies you develop will bear a direct relationship to the image you are building. You must consider carefully how these strategies work separately (when directed at discrete target markets) and how they work collectively (what synergy you can expect as one "piggy-backs" another). You must also consider strategies in relation to competition.

A marketing model for image building

Figure 6 shows a conceptual and practical marketing model for institutional image building, adapted from "The Communications Process in Marketing" developed by the Barton-Gillet Company. The model relates two very simple concepts: receiver attitudes and communication methods.

Across the top are states of mind of your target audience members regarding your institution and its programs. These fall on a scale of intensity ranging from *awareness* (at left) to *commitment* (right). Imagine a member of your target audience

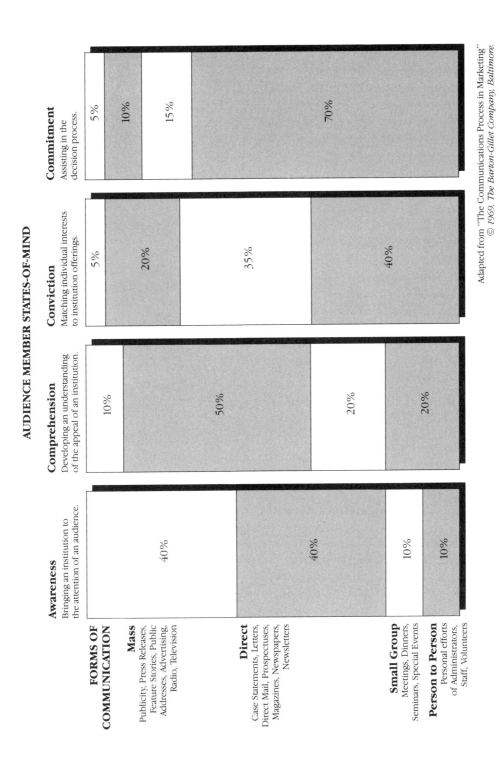

Figure 6: A Marketing Model

at some point on the scale. He or she may be at the low end of the scale—at *awareness.* This person would have some knowledge of your institution, programs, or activities. The target audience member may have positive feelings, negative feelings, or no feelings at all about your institution. The scale continues through *comprehension* to *conviction* and peaks at *commitment.* These states of mind relate closely to image concepts.

By communicating to members of your target audience, you can move them across this horizontal scale. The vertical scale on the left side of the model describes various forms of communications you might use to do this. The model illustrates how your media mix must become more personal as an audience member approaches *commitment.*

Forms of communications are grouped into clusters with percentages assigned to each. These percentages are intended as rough guides to the degree you should use each form of communication for a particular audience group. The four methods of communications—mass, direct, small group, and person to person—include various media forms and communications vehicles.

Use the chart to select the most effective and efficient communications mix to achieve a desired state of mind in a target audience.

For example, if your institutional image marketing objective is to achieve *awareness* in your target audience, then mass media and direct are the best forms of communication. On the other hand, if your institutional image marketing objective is to achieve *commitment,* mass media is not the best form of communication; person-to-person contact is.

Remember, audiences move across the scale slowly. An institution cannot "rocket" an audience member from the low end to the high end. To achieve an institutional image objective requires carefully planned, research-based, deliberate, repeated efforts.

The art of planning ahead

Wouldn't it be great if you could see into the future and anticipate reactions or events? You could achieve greater impact and better institutional image results if you could predict what people will say, do, or think about your efforts. It would help you decide what to do and how to do it, and it would help to ensure success.

There *are* ways to predict how people will react to ideas, events, and activities. There's no magic about it. You can develop these skills to help you in your work.

We learn early in life how to plan, and we plan many things. We plan projects, activities, vacations, meals, when to sleep, when to wake up, and where to go. Planning takes a certain amount of imagination. We visualize in our minds what we want to do, we create a mental plan, and then we do it.

Unfortunately, most of us are simply content to enjoy the results of these short-term mental efforts. We do not add a step to that process: we don't use imagination to help us project into or anticipate the future.

When we combine imaginative planning with the creativity of new ideas we

56

begin to develop insight into the future. We can, for instance, plan an image program. We can do that mentally, verbally, or in writing. We can then project that image program into the future by using our imagination. We can predict many things about that image program—what problems might develop, what the most successful outcomes might be.

For example, suppose you are asked to help your institution's president prepare a speech for an alumni group in another state. You could begin by calling some influential alumni who live there. You could ask them what issues or ideas they've discussed at their alumni meetings. You could gather demographic information (ages, income levels, business interests, sex).

Once you have this data, you could use it to target interesting and related image-building information. Assemble the ideas into some overall concepts for the president to consider. Then "brainstorm" with the president. How would this speech help your institution's image? How would particular ideas be received? What outcomes can you anticipate? How do these outcomes relate to other institutional plans and objectives?

There are a few things you need in order to use a crystal ball effectively.

Start with history. The best way to develop insight is to look at the past. You need to understand the history of whatever it is you are planning. Reading, research, and investigation will provide an information base. Ask others about the past and keep a mental or written file of historical information. For instance, you may discover that your institution's image derives from some specific past actions. You must take this into account in planning for your new image.

For example, for many years I was employed by Wright State University in Dayton, Ohio. Wright State was one of the youngest institutions in the Ohio State System. The university was named after Orville and Wilbur Wright, Dayton residents and inventors of the first flying machine. This relationship of institution to historical people and events provided a wealth of editorial and visual material that we used to build an image for the institution. That image suggested a long-term stability, despite our status as the "new kid" on the academic block. By making this association with the past, we were able to create a subtle but powerful image for the present and future.

Once you have gathered as much information as you can, apply it in your planning. This can be a mental process. You first use your imagination to visualize the plan. Then use creativity to project your plans into the future. Apply the historical facts, research, and information you have gathered and visualize people, their ideas, possible reactions and comments. You can then anticipate results. This is called *creative planning*. You can develop plans, modify them mentally, and refine them to get the best results. If you do this regularly, you will find that you can anticipate more and more complex situations. You can refine the historical fact-gathering and research process and develop sophisticated libraries of information, eventually building a powerful mental (or computerized!) information base that you can apply to current and future activities.

As you plan, it's vital that you keep in mind the outcome you want to achieve. Figure 7 illustrates the process of responding to audience needs with appropri-

Figure 7: Responding to Audience Needs

ate institutional offerings. This *exchange* process is a basic marketing concept.

For instance, alumni may donate money in exchange for the satisfaction of knowing that a capital campaign will help their institution. This process yields consumer satisfaction and assists in image building. It applies equally to admissions, fund raising, alumni work, grant proposal preparation, community relations, and many other areas of activity in higher education. Keep this concept in mind when you plan ahead. If you know your audience's needs, you can plan activities or programs with those needs in mind.

The role of image marketing

As educational institutions move toward new challenges, many will begin to look to image building and marketing to bring a new system of order to their activities. Marketing is an effective tool to communicate important concepts to internal staffs as well as to external constituents. It is organized, planned, researched, thoughtful, controlled application of ideas to achieve greater results than could otherwise be possible.

In the past, higher education was perceived as a homogenous conglomerate. Some institutions maintained distinct positions, but this occurred more by accident than by plan. Today, with increasing competition for students, funds, and resources, institutions can no longer afford to be misunderstood, ignored, overlooked, or confused with competing institutions.

How consumers (and all constituents) perceive your institution of higher education is becoming more and more critical. Your role in that process is critical as well. Perceptions are powerful—sometimes more powerful than fact. You must be able to differentiate your institution positively from its competitors. Educational institutions have begun to realize that successful image development is an outgrowth of effective marketing. It can help them advance on many fronts.

This publication has described ways you can apply image building and related marketing concepts to benefit your educational institution. The rest is up to you.

Part IV

Appendix

Glossary

Acronym
A word formed from the initial letters of an institution or activity, such as OSU from Ohio State University or NCAA from National Collegiate Athletic Association.

Audit
A review and analysis of tangible and/or intangible elements that project an institution's image.

Clarifier
A word or phrase added to an institution's name to more clearly communicate information about the institution.

Comparative differential advantage
The most positive or outstanding aspects of an institution's programs, activities, and services, as determined by research. This advantage forms the focus of an image program. From a constituent's point of view, the comparative differential advantage is the institution's set of qualities that stands out favorably when judged against those of competing institutions.

Constituent
A person or set of people served by, associated with, or in contact with an institution; a part of a larger whole. Examples of an educational institution's constituencies include students, faculty, staff, donors, alumni, prospective students, parents, corporations and foundations, community members, and other friends of the institution.

Demographics
The statistical study of a population; the sets of characteristics that distinguish segments of an audience. Examples are age, sex, education, occupation, geographic distribution, giving habits, lifestyle, and so on.

Global institutional image or *umbrella image*
The image of an entire institution, as perceived by all of its constituencies. Global institutional image combines the individual images of each aspect or component of the institution into a collective image.

Hierarchical structure
The arrangement of components at different levels within a parent organization (e.g., courses in a department, departments in a college, colleges in a university).

Identity
The state in which an institution's reality matches audience perceptions of it.

Image
The aggregate, or sum, of feelings, beliefs, attitudes, impressions, thoughts, perceptions, ideas, recollections, conclusions, and mind sets someone has about an institution, its components, or its products.

Image enhancement
Emphasizing carefully considered aspects or features of an institution (or its subunits) to create a more positive position for it in the perceiver's mind.

Image lag
The difference between reality and a person's perceptions, caused by changes during the time that has elapsed since the perceptions were formed.

Image link
Synergistic influences among groups and individuals that affect their perceptions of a common subject.

Image onion
An analogy illustrating that perceptions of a product become less accurate and less precise as viewer contact with the product becomes more distant.

Marketing
The research, planning, and presentation of tangible or intangible products to target audiences in order to achieve planned, coordinated results.

Marketing mix
The blending of marketing principles and practices to achieve planned results.

Media mix
The combination of specific communications forms (press releases, newsletters, speeches, advertisements, direct mailers, etc.) selected as best suited to achieving specific marketing objectives.

Perception
The process by which a person becomes aware of, observes, and attempts to understand reality, and the knowledge or awareness produced by this process.

Position
The relationship of your institution and its products to competing institutions and their products, as perceived by constituents.

Positioning
The process of adjusting constituents' perceptions of an institution and its products to achieve a specific position in relation to competitors.

Product
A tangible or intangible item offered to satisfy consumer needs.

Product differentiation
The use of a product's characteristics to distinguish a product from competing products in the minds of target audience members.

Research
Systematic investigation, measurement, and compilation of information in order to form new ideas or to verify existing ideas.

Stimulus
An action, especially a communication, meant to cause a reaction or response.

Strategy
The art and science of adapting and coordinating research and resources to attain marketing objectives.

Target audience
One segment of a larger population group (called a universe), defined by demographics or other factors.

Bibliography

Basic marketing texts

Kotler, Philip. *Marketing for Nonprofit Organizations.* Englewood Cliffs, N.J.: Prentice-Hall, 1975; revised 1982. One of the best books describing marketing and image-building techniques for nonprofit organizations, written by a professor at Northwestern University. In an easy-to-read style, Kotler describes marketing techniques and ways to apply them to higher education and other nonprofit organizations.

Kotler, Philip, and Fox, Karen F. A. *Strategic Marketing for Educational Institutions.* Englewood Cliffs, N.J.: Prentice-Hall, 1985. This book examines marketing concepts and tools for administrators in colleges, universities, and private schools. The book's strategic planning perspective, numerous examples, and careful organization helps advancement professionals apply marketing and image-building concepts to their institutions.

Topor, Robert S. *Marketing Higher Education: A Practical Guide.* Washington, D.C.: Council for Advancement and Support of Education, 1983. Designed for the newcomer to institutional marketing, this guide describes how to apply marketing concepts and techniques. The book helps advancement professionals analyze target audience needs; improve products, services, and communications; and become more effective administrators. Subjects covered include marketing strategies, research, services, events, communications, image perception, audience segmentation, and positioning.

Other marketing and institutional image references

Adler, Mortimer T. *How to Speak/How to Listen.* New York: Macmillan, 1983.

Bagozzi, Richard. *Marketing in the 80's: Changes and Challenges.* Chicago: American Marketing Association, 1980.

Barton-Gillet Company. "The Communications Process in Marketing." Baltimore: 1969.

Bennett, Claude. *Reflective Appraisal of Programs.* Ithaca: Cornell University Media Services, 1982.

Berlo, David K. *The Process of Communication.* New York: Holt, Rinehart and Winston, 1960.

Blankenship, A.B. *Professional Telephone Surveys.* New York: McGraw-Hill, 1977.

Bogart, Leo. *Strategy in Advertising.* New York: Harcourt, Brace and World, 1967.

Boone, Louis E., and Kurtz, David L. *Contemporary Marketing.* Hinsdale, Ill.: The Dryden Press, 1977.

Cetron, Marvin, and O'Toole, Thomas. *Encounters with the Future: A Forecast of Life into the 21st Century.* New York: McGraw-Hill, 1972.

Cochran, William C. *Sampling Techniques,* 2nd edition. New York: John Wiley & Sons, 1963.

Council for Advancement and Support of Education. "What Is Market Research? What Can It Do for Me?" CASE CURRENTS, May/June, 1982.

Crane, Edgar. *Marketing Communications.* New York: John Wiley & Sons, 1972.

Dillman, Don A. *Mail and Telephone Surveys: The Total Design Method.* New York: John Wiley & Sons, 1978.

Erdos, Paul. *Professional Mail Surveys.* New York: McGraw-Hill, 1970.

Ferber, Robert, ed. *Handbook of Marketing Research.* New York: McGraw-Hill, 1974.

Fine, Seymour H. *The Marketing of Ideas and Social Issues.* New York: Praeger Publishers, 1981.

Flint, Emily P., ed. *Creative Editing and Writing Workbook.* Washington, D.C.: Council for Advancement and Support of Education, 1979.

Fowler, Charles R. "Making Marketing Work: How a coordinated approach improved a college's enrollment, retention, and public image." CURRENTS, November/December 1983, pp. 20-22.

Francis, J. Bruce, ed. *Surveying Institutional Constituencies.* Washington, D.C.: Jossey-Bass, 1979.

Goldstein, Sherry, and Kravetz, Ellen, eds. *Findex: The Directory of Market Research Reports, Studies and Surveys, 5th edition.* New York: Find/SVP, 1983.

Group Attitudes Corporation. *American Attitudes Toward Higher Education,* 2 vols. New York: Hill & Knowlton, 1982, 1983, 1984.

Ihlanfeldt, William. "A Management Approach to the Buyer's Market." *Liberal Education*, May 1975, pp. 133-148.

Kotler, Philip. *Marketing Management: Analysis, Planning and Control*, 3rd edition. Englewood Cliffs, N.J.: Prentice-Hall, 1976.

Kotler, Philip, et al. *Cases and Readings for Marketing for Nonprofit Organizations*. Englewood Cliffs, N.J.: Prentice-Hall, 1983.

Kress, George. *Marketing Research,* 2nd edition. Reston, Va.: Reston Publishing Co., 1982.

Levitt, Theodore. "Marketing Myopia." *Harvard Business Review,* July/August 1960, pp. 45-56.

Lindenmann, Walter K. *Attitude and Opinion Research: Why You Need It/How to Do It,* 3rd edition. Washington, D.C.: Council for Advancement and Support of Education, 1983.

Lovelock, Christopher H., and Weinberg, Charles B. *Marketing for Public and Nonprofit Managers.* New York: John Wiley & Sons, 1984.

McMillan, Norman H. *Marketing Your Hospital: A Strategy for Survival.* Chicago: American Hospital Association, 1981.

Moll, Richard W. "A Flower Child Grows Up: Responding to changing times at UC Santa Cruz." CURRENTS, November/December 1983, pp. 16-18.

Nie, Norman, et al. *SPSS,* 2nd edition. New York: McGraw-Hill, 1975.

Opinion Research Corporation. *American Attitudes Toward Higher Education.* New York: 1985.

Payne, Stanley. *The Art of Asking Questions.* Princeton: Princeton University Press, 1954.

Ries, Al, and Trout, Jack. *Positioning: The Battle for Your Mind.* New York: McGraw-Hill, 1981.

Rogers, Everett M., and Shoemaker, F. Floyd. *Communication of Innovations.* New York: The Free Press, 1971.

Roman, Kenneth, and Maas, Jane. *How to Advertise.* New York: St. Martin's Press, 1977.

Rowland, A. Westley. *Handbook of Institutional Advancement.* San Francisco: Jossey-Bass, 1978. (Revised edition being published in 1986.)

Selame, Elinor, and Selame, Joe. *Developing a Corporate Identity.* New York: Lebhar-Friedman Books, 1980.

Topor, Robert S. *Marketing Cooperative Extension.* Ithaca: Cornell University Media Services, 1982.

Udell, Jon G., and Laczniak, Gene R. *Marketing in an Age of Change.* New York: John Wiley & Sons, 1981.

U.S. Department of Commerce, Bureau of Economic Analysis. *Business Conditions Digest.* Washington, D.C.: U.S. Government Printing Office, monthly.

West, Christopher. *Marketing on a Small Budget.* New York: John Wiley & Sons, 1975.

About
the Author

Robert Topor

Robert Topor began working in university advancement while an undergraduate at Syracuse University. He received his bachelor's degree in advertising and journalism from Syracuse in 1958 and then worked as a graphic designer for Syracuse University Press before entering the military.

While in the Army, Topor was stationed at White Sands Missile Range, New Mexico. He supervised a technical illustration section, and he and his staff prepared illustrations and animation for public information and missile research films.

In 1962, he returned to Syracuse University where he worked as production manager in the printing division.

In 1963, Topor accepted a position in the public relations department of the University of Rochester. For 11 years he worked closely with alumni, admissions, and development staffs, designing materials for the university, Strong Memorial Hospital, the Eastman School of Music, and the Memorial Art Gallery. He received his master's degree from the University of Rochester in 1971.

Topor moved to Princeton, New Jersey, in 1974 to serve as creative manager for Peterson's Guides, where he worked closely with many schools, community colleges, universities, and colleges in the Northeast.

In 1975, he became director of university publications at Wright State University in Dayton, Ohio. At Wright State, he developed institutional advancement plans for development, admissions, and alumni activities.

Topor began working as a senior administrator for Cornell University Media Services in Ithaca, New York, in 1979. While at Cornell, he wrote a guidebook describing ways to apply marketing ideas for Cornell Cooperative Extension, a nonprofit educational network in New York State. His marketing concepts have been used by many other state cooperative extension systems.

In 1983 he was appointed director of publications and graphics for the Sharp HealthCare system in San Diego, California. In 1985, he became director of marketing promotion. He works in the public affairs and fund-raising departments. At Sharp, Topor has been involved in planning and implementing system-wide graphics standards and a corporate marketing and image-building plan. He also serves as a communications and marketing consultant for numerous higher education institutions.

A frequent and popular speaker in the United States and Canada for the Council for Advancement and Support of Education (CASE), Topor has delivered talks on marketing, admissions, and publications. He chaired CASE's Marketing for Student Recruitment summer institutes at the University of New Hampshire in 1981 and at the University of Maryland in 1983. In 1983, CASE published Topor's book *Marketing Higher Education: A Practical Guide.*

The recipient of many professional awards and recognitions, Topor is a dedicated teacher and practitioner of marketing and its application to nonprofit organizations and institutions.